The Merrill Studies
in
An American Tragedy

CHARLES E. MERRILL STUDIES

Under the General Editorship of
Matthew J. Bruccoli and Joseph Katz

The Merrill Studies
in
An American Tragedy

Compiled by

Jack Salzman

Long Island University

Charles E. Merrill Publishing Company
A Bell & Howell Company
Columbus, Ohio

ISBN: 0-675-9205-1

Library of Congress Catalog Card Number: 70-150995

1 2 3 4 5 6 7 — 77 76 75 74 73 72 71

Printed in the United States of America

Preface

In the summer of 1905 word came from a small town near Big Moose Lake, in upper New York State, of a young man and woman who had drowned in the lake. At first, nothing was found but an upturned boat and a floating straw hat. Then the lake was dragged and the body of Grace (Billy) Brown was discovered. Shortly after, the man, Chester Gillette, was also located, only he was discovered among a fairly exclusive camping party on one of the adjacent lakes. Gillette, it was learned, was the nephew of a collar factory owner in Cortland, New York, where both he and Billy Brown had been employed. Gillette's room was searched and a bundle of Billy's letters was uncovered. They revealed that Billy and Chester Gillette not only had been lovers but that Billy was pregnant and wanted Gillette to marry her. (In her last letter to him, an apparently desperate Billy Brown threatened that unless Chester married her right away she would expose her lover before all his "fine friends.") On the basis of this evidence—and a bruise on Billy's forehead—Chester Gillette was indicted for murder and, after a trial which received extensive newspaper coverage, was found guilty. He was electrocuted at Auburn Penitentiary in March 1908.

The Chester Gillette-Billy Brown case became the immediate source for *An American Tragedy*, the most monumental of all Dreiser's novels, which Horace Liveright published in a two volume set in December, 1925. However, the Big Moose Lake murder was by no means Dreiser's only source. As early as

1892, when he was starting his career as a newspaperman, Dreiser began to observe a certain type of crime in the United States which, as he wrote in 1935, "seemed to spring from the fact that almost every young person was possessed of an ingrowing ambition to be somebody financially and socially."[1] The mood of America, Dreiser was convinced, was directed toward escape from any form of poverty. As a result, the accumulation of wealth had come to denote power, social superiority, even social domination. The ideals of life, liberty, and the pursuit of happiness had become no more than clichés; the ambitious American (to paraphrase H. Rap Brown) had made murder as American as apple pie. Dreiser's own account of his growing awareness of the distortion of the American dream, here quoted in part, is most revealing for what it tells us about his concerns in *An American Tragedy*:

Most men, as I found [Dreiser wrote], were neither patriots nor advocates of liberty for others, nor were they even fair-minded. Life was a struggle for existence, and a cruel struggle. To be sure, there was operating a so-called social system which sought by law at least to enforce some measure of honesty and fairness. But as to the working of the same, how different! In every town and city with which I came in contact, the well-to-do dominated the less well-to-do, and to the general disadvantage of the latter. The rich controlled whatever industries there were and fixed all too often the most exacting and not infrequently slave-like hour and wage terms. Altogether, pride and show, and even waste, were flaunted in a new and still fairly virgin land—in the face of poverty and want, and not poverty and want on the part of those who would not work, but the poverty and want of those who were all too eager to work, and almost on any terms.

In other words, I was witnessing the upbuilding of the great American fortunes. And once these fortunes and the families which controlled them were established, there began to develop our 'leisure class,' the Four Hundred of New York and the slave aristocracy of the South, plus their imitators in the remainder of the states. And this class, as I studied it, presented the very interesting thought that all of its heirs and assigns were not so much interested in work or mental or national development in any

---

[1] All quotations, unless otherwise noted, are from Dreiser's article, "I Find the Real American Tragedy," *The Mystery Magazine*, XI (February 1935), 10-11, 88-90. Reprinted by permission of Harold J. Dies, trustee for the Dreiser trust.

form as they were in leisure and show—the fanfare and parade of wealth without any consideration for the workers from whom it was taken or the country as a whole. I saw also that the maintaining of those privileges was likewise the principal business of those who were not heirs to anything—the young and ambitious in nearly all walks of life. In fact, between 1875 and 1900 it became an outstanding American madness which led first to the great war of 1914–18 and culminated finally in the financial debacle of 1929.

Indeed, throughout this period, as I found, it was the rare American heart that was set, for instance, on being a great scientist, discover, religionist, philosopher, or benefactor to mankind in any form. True enough, a man might start out to be a doctor, a lawyer, a merchant, an inventor, perhaps even a scientist, but his private obsession, due to the national obsession which I have just described, was that the quick and sure way to do this was to get money. And one of the quickest ways to get money was to marry it, not develop oneself and so have money come honestly. In short, we bred the fortune hunter de luxe. Fortune-hunting became a disease. Hence, my first notice of and interest in this particular type of crime first mentioned.

By the time he came to write *An American Tragedy*, Dreiser had many crimes of this particular type to select as his model. In 1893, for example, there had been the case of Carlyle Harris, a medical student who used poisoned powder to murder the girl he had seduced. Then in 1899 had come the Richard Molyneux case, in 1911 the Avis Linnell-Clarence Richesen case, and in 1916 the Orpet case. Most of these murders, which Dreiser followed avidly in the newspapers, involved the killing of a young woman by an ambitious young man. In the Albert T. Patrick case, however, Dreiser found an instance of an attorney who had murdered his wealthy and aged client. And yet a third variant which Dreiser observed was that "of the ambitious young lover of some poorer girl, who in the earlier state of his affairs had been attractive enough to satisfy him both in the matter of love and her social station. But nearly always with the passing of time and the growth of experience on the part of the youth, a more attractive girl with money or position appeared and he quickly discovered that he could no longer care for his first love." And if, as in the case of Chester Gillette and Billy Brown, it was not possible for the young man to drop the first girl, murder "became more and more common."

In part, Dreiser finally settled upon the Gillette-Brown murder as his basic source for *An American Tragedy* because the details of the case were most accessible to him. But, even more important, Gillette's life seemed to Dreiser to epitomize the American tragedy. For if Gillette was a murderer, he was just as much the victim of a distorted social dream. Gillette's hope of connecting himself with what he considered to be the superior life of his uncle impressed Dreiser as having a clear tie "with the general social and financial attitudes of Americans—their dreams of grandeur, all based on financial advancement." By American standards, there certainly was nothing antisocial about Gillette's aspirations. If anything, Dreiser wrote, "He was really doing the kind of thing which Americans should and would have said was the wise and moral thing for him to do had he not committed a murder." Nor was Gillette's instinct that of a criminal: he was simply too young, too inexperienced, too underdeveloped mentally to be the deliberate author of an antisocial murder. Gillette wanted only to escape from the circumstances which had made it impossible for him to fulfill the dreams instilled in him by the American system, and for this he was executed. In short, the murderer was himself murdered by the very system whose values he exemplified.

Dreiser stayed fairly close to his sources in writing *An American Tragedy*; he made extensive use, for example, of both the letters Billy Brown wrote to Chester Gillette and the transcript of Gillette's trial. But *An American Tragedy* is hardly a mere reworking of the newspaper accounts of the Big Moose Lake murder, as has too often been asserted. Not only had Dreiser begun preparations for *An American Tragedy* some years before the drowning of Grace Brown, as his papers in a file entitled "The Rake" make clear;[2] but many of the "facts" and almost all of the characterizations are a product not of newspaper accounts but of Dreiser's imagination. Clyde Griffiths's childhood, for example, is much closer to that of Dreiser himself than it is to that of Gillette; and, in general, Clyde is considerably less sophisticated than Gillette apparently was. The newspaper accounts, moreover, had virtually nothing to report about the debutante who was the prototype of Sondra Finchley. And, of considerable impor-

---

[2] For an account of the writing of *An American Tragedy* see Robert Elias, *Theodore Dreiser: Apostle of Nature* (New York: Knopf, 1948) and Ellen Moers, *Two Dreisers* (New York: Viking, 1969).

tance, Dreiser deliberately changed the circumstances surrounding Grace Brown's death. The most damaging evidence against Chester Gillette had been the inexplicable presence of a tennis racket which Gillette allegedly had taken with him when he and Billy had gone rowing; the racket purportedly had caused the bruise which was found on the forehead of the dead girl. Clyde, however, takes a camera with him, which by its plausibility considerably vitiates the contention of a premeditated murder. In addition, Dreiser does not show Clyde actually drowning Roberta Alden, but has him watch as she drowns after the boat has accidentally tipped. Thus, just as he had introduced the element of chance into George Hurstwood's theft of the money in *Sister Carrie*, so in *An American Tragedy* he creates a situation where the guilt of an individual cannot be decided with the certainty of the jury which had condemned Chester Gillette to death: "There are decisions," Dreiser told a reporter for the *Denver Post* in November, 1926, "which casually chosen juries of men, unused to judge human motives and actions, are ludicrously unfit to render."[3] Chester Gillette, as some contemporary reports had it, may have confessed his guilt before his execution. But Dreiser does not have Clyde confess; there may have been murder in his heart, as Clyde admits to Reverend McMillan, but that is all. If Clyde Griffiths is guilty, he is no more guilty than the jury which convicts him.

The publication of *An American Tragedy* in 1925 afforded Dreiser his first real financial and critical success. From the time of the publication of his first novel, *Sister Carrie*, in 1900, Dreiser's writings had been received with a mixed reaction. Yet by 1925 he had come to be regarded as one of America's foremost writers. Much of his reputation, however, was based on the social importance of his novels rather than on their literary quality. *Sister Carrie* had been a landmark in the fight against the Genteel Tradition in American letters; and in 1916, *The "Genius,"* Dreiser's last major work before the publication of *An American Tragedy*, was withdrawn by the publisher because obscenity charges had been levied against it. (A petition objecting to the banning of *The "Genius"* by The New York Society for the Suppression of Vice was signed by almost 500 writers, but the novel remained unavail-

---

[3] Quoted in Elias, p. 223.

able until 1923.) Dreiser was being talked about but his novels were not being read. Then came *An American Tragedy*. H. L. Mencken, one of Dreiser's earliest champions, didn't like it very much, nor did Robert Benchley, who wrote a devastating satire for *Life Magazine*. But most of the reviews were extremely favorable—including the one by Dreiser's old and formidable nemesis, Stuart Sherman—and *An American Tragedy* quickly became the best known of Dreiser's novels. It remains the work by which Dreiser is most popularly known, no doubt due in part to the Hollywood films which have been made of it.

An American Tragedy, of course, still has its detractors. Lionel Trilling and, more recently, Charles Thomas Samuels continue to deride Dreiser's art ("Dreiser lacked more than art," Samuels has written; "he lacked a sense of what he lacked."). Yet, as the following reviews and essays make clear, *An American Tragedy* not only is the best known of Dreiser's works; it is also the most highly esteemed. "It is a masterpiece, nothing less," Irving Howe wrote recently. And it is in large part due to *An American Tragedy* that Dreiser, to quote Howe again, "ranks among the American giants, the very few American giants we have had."

J. S.

Contents

1. Reviews

2. Studies

The Merrill Studies
in
An American Tragedy

1. Reviews

Dreiser

Theodore Dreiser—what a man—what a huge figure on the American scene.

There are certain American men I myself have met and am glad to have met, Mr. Dreiser, Henry Mencken, Clarence Darrow, Stark Young, Alfred Kreymborg, Alfred Stieglitz, John Marin. There are a dozen others, all notable American men to me.

America has many men of note just now, walking about, doing their work, helping to mold our minds. How clearly Dreiser stands out among them all. There will not be another like him here. He is to my mind the biggest, most important American of our times. As a writer the man is often crude, dull sometimes with unbelievable dulness, honest, tender. His tenderness is the finest thing of all. How can anyone—a writer like myself—help being sorry his tenderness does not run out more directly toward words? Surely the man does not love words as words. He is so often unbelievably brutal with them. I pick up this new, big novel of his, "An American Tragedy," and on every page there are sentences that make me cringe, words that make me cringe.

It is Christmas morning in New Orleans and I have been all morning reading Dreiser's new novel and Amy Lowell's "John Keats"—going from one to the other. They are both unfinished as I sit writing. What a fine sensual love of words in Miss Lowell. What a lack of it in Dreiser. But what corking American writers. American writing was never so fine as it is now. Do you believe with me that Mr. Theodore Dreiser is more responsible for that fact than any other American? I get it very keenly as I sit writing this article. Miss Lowell of Massachusetts—Dreiser of Indiana.

In New Orleans—in the poorer section where I live—the neighbors all get drunk on Christmas. A drunken man, in sport, has just taken all his wife's best clothes down into the yard and soused them in a washtub. Now she will have to stay home all day and take care of him. He laughs hoarsely. The wife laughs and swears.

These are Dreiser's kind of people—these in their grim and gay moments. Common Americans, undistinguished. What a lot of them. How the man Dreiser has loved and understood them.

Reprinted from *The Saturday Review of Literature,* II (January 9, 1926), 475, by permission of *Saturday Review.*

And yet look what the man does. Right at the beginning of this new big book—on page ten—read this. He is describing his hero's father:

> To begin with, Asa Griffiths, the father, was one of those poorly integrated and correlated organisms, the product of an environment and a religious theory, but with no guiding or mental insight of his own, yet sensitive and therefore highly emotional, and without any practical sense whatsoever.

"No guiding or mental insight of his own." Great God! One's mind jumps away to other fellows of the ink-pots—say George Moore in the "Brook Kerith," Stark Young's jeweled clearness, Henry Mencken's gay word rattling, Mr. Stuart Sherman's solid prose.

Plenty of word lovers in the world, loving words, slinging ink. But Dreiser isn't one of them. If you look for word-love in his book you'll get left. Love of human beings you'll find. It's a finer attribute in the end. Lay your Dreiser book over against the book of any of the modern "smarties" among our writers and you'll understand. You'll understand also why all men here who care about writing care so much for Dreiser.

You go on for endless pages of dulness with Dreiser, like walking on the prairies, say of the Dakotas or in the desert country, endless piling up of heavy cumbersome sentences, something level and low, with a dreary sameness you think at first will drive you mad.

If you think you are going to escape Dreiser by realizing he can be dull you are mistaken. He'll get you in the end. Buy this book and read it all. Don't be finicky. It will reward you as every book of Dreiser's always does. You'll never get the beauty of the prairies or the desert by being mincing and finicky. They are beautiful. So is Dreiser and his work. You have to pay for beauty. Pay for it in Dreiser by going right on through with him. Take along water, bread, and wine. Prepare for a journey you'll never forget. Take a day off, two days, a week. Go up into the country for a week-end alone—take Dreiser's two volumes with you on a train journey. Find out, once for all, the difference between a human flesh and blood, male man, full of real tenderness for life, and the smarties, the word slingers, the clever fellows, the nasty cocksure half men of the writing world.

All that Dreiser misses in feeling for words, sentences, the page of the book, he pours out into tenderness for people. He goes with his people into every little detail of their lives. The drama grows slowly bigger and bigger. A Dreiser book—Dreiser's people—you never forget. That's a lot. That's everything. That's what makes Dreiser what he is—the most important American writing. More than that—the most important man writing English.

I'll not go on any more about Dreiser's bad sentences. You'll find them on every page of his book like sage brush on the desert. You go around anywhere in America where men and women who care about writing get together and you'll hear the same thing. Everyone begins by speaking of the terrible sentences of Dreiser. Then they speak of other things for a time and come back to the man Dreiser. Tenderness creeps into voices. Every writing man and woman in America who really cares about writing loves this man. And it isn't Dreiser, the human social being, they love. He keeps himself to himself, is that odd thing among writers, a truly modest man. What other American writers love is Theodore Dreiser the writer as he is in "An American Tragedy," with all of his sins on his head, just as he always is.

I am not going to try to talk of these two new volumes in detail. Frankly I haven't had time to read them enough for that and I won't be hurried. And anyway, you can't get at Dreiser that way. Buy and read "An American Tragedy." Stand the two volumes upon your shelves. An American library without Dreiser complete is just no library at all—at least not an American library.

It comes to this—that the great human tenderness of Dreiser, that has got into his work in spite of his word heaviness, is in "An American Tragedy." There is no smartness, no cleverness. There is just the man we American writers love and respect above all other writing artists here—the biggest man we've had. And that's enough.

Get and read "An American Tragedy" for yourself if you have any feeling for American writing. That's all I can say.

Touching a Terrible Tragedy

I finished Theodore Dreiser's latest story just before going to bed last night. I assume that I must have had some sleep during the troubled hours through which I tossed and dreamed after laying it down. But the haunted face of a helpless boy, strapped to an iron chair at Sing Sing, and the wan form of a dead girl floating on a lonely black lake surrounded by tall pine trees in Northern New York still were haunting me when I awoke. I presume the feeling will slowly fade from my consciousness and be blended with the other experiences, painful and pleasant, which make up life. I hardly can think of the eight hundred pages of "An American Tragedy" as a book. It does not leave the impression that goes with reading a story; the feeling is rather that of a series of terrible physical impacts that have relentlessly shocked every sensitive nerve in the body.

Clyde Griffiths was born in Kansas City. His father was an ignorant, zealous street preacher, who thought that the chief concern, if not the only one, of life was to praise God and leave your fate in His hands. He had a wife and three woebegone children, whom he kept in a weird and crazy mission house. The main room was filled with the misfits and half-wits that always gather in such places to get warm and listen to the senseless ravings in which the congregation are told that if they give themselves to God they are the elect of the world. In the daytime the father takes a small hand organ and a few hymn books and, with his wife and pathetic children, goes up and down the busy streets, singing and praying and calling the people to repent. Of course, only weaklings follow him, but still he believes he is important to the scheme of salvation and steadily keeps on his way. The children are brought up without education, knowledge or experience. Clyde soon grows ashamed of the grotesque family and the mean home. The boys shun him and laugh at him, and the girls do not even know that he is there. So he leaves the back bedroom,

Reprinted from the *New York Evening Post Literary Review*, January 16, 1926, pp. 1-2.

rickety furniture and weird aggregation that he calls home and
gets a job as a bellhop in a big hotel.

Clyde is a bellhop in his teens and is neither good nor bad. He
has been told nothing of life, has no education and is in no way
adjusted to the world. He is attractive, sensitive, impressionable
and weak. In short, not different from 90 per cent of all the millions
that make up the population of the earth.

Without the slightest preparation, he faces puberty, with all of
its new emotions and luring calls. All he knows is learned from the
visits of bellhops to hotel rooms and the companions that a boy in
such surroundings ordinarily meets. The conversations of the bellboys in the big hotel largely concern sex and tips. Clyde's social
life is made up of his companions and their sisters and the shop-
girls that are naturally thrown in his way. Mr. Dreiser evidently
has gone to great pains correctly to know this sort of life. And the
life of the hotel from the view of the bellhop has its interest, the
same as life from any other angle.

In spite of goodly tips, his love of girls and clothes keep him in
debt, and this is increased by helping his mother protect a sister
who, to escape her wretched home, fled with a lover who soon left
her with a baby in her arms. Clyde always found it hard to say no,
especially to a girl who used her blandishments to coax money
from him to buy hats and ribbons and such finery as would make
her still more tempting to Clyde and his friends.

One day Clyde was asked by his companions to attend a wild
picnic in the country. This was made more alluring because one
of the boys had a chance to borrow a fine car from his employer,
who was away from home. It was late in the afternoon before they
started back. The usual delays of blocked traffic, flat tires and
detours made them late. The rules for reporting at the hotel in
time to go on duty were very strict. In a panic, they increased
their speed and the car ran over a little girl at a street crossing.
The driver, realizing what had happened, madly sped through
town to escape the pursuing police. The car was overturned and
the occupants fled in every direction. Clyde made his escape on a
freight train and, after severe hardships, turned up two years later
in Chicago, a waiter in the Union League Club.

Clyde had often heard his father tell of a rich brother who was
a large manufacturer of collars in Lycurgus, N. Y. One day this
uncle came to Chicago and stopped at the Union League Club. As
fate would have it, Clyde was assigned to take his uncle's meals

to his room. The relationship was discovered and the uncle was much impressed with the politeness and intelligence of the boy.

In due course Clyde was offered work in the great collar factory and, of course, eagerly accepted the chance. On arriving at the factory he was sent to his cousin, who resented his coming and gave him one of the hardest jobs in the place. Later his uncle interfered to offer him a little better chance as foreman of the marking room, where all the employees were girls. One of these, brighter and more attractive than the rest, soon impressed the foreman. Clyde was lonely in his new environment. His rich relatives made no effort to help him or introduce him into the life of the community. They thought they had done their duty when they gave him a place and once asked him to dine with the family. Here, by chance, he met an attractive girl, Sondra Finchley, a member of one of the leading families of the town. Clyde was smitten with her beauty, vivacity and costume.

Under these circumstances his interest in the employee, Roberta, rapidly waned. It was necessary that his meetings with Roberta should be clandestine. This finally resulted in his habitually going to her room. Both were lonely and the result was easy to foresee. By another chance he again met Sondra, who was much impressed with his easy manners and attractive appearance. This soon brought him in contact with the social leaders of the town and the acquaintance ripened into a serious love affair. Clyde's salary was small and was easily engulfed in the demand for clothes and haberdashery, made necessary to keep up the pace.

It was not long until Roberta was terrified with the knowledge that she was on the way to becoming a mother. In the meantime Clyde's desire was to marry Sondra, whose beauty and culture, together with her prospects, opened a wide and attractive field for his growing love and ambition. Clyde's problem was to release himself in some way from Roberta, and her condition made the tangle a desperate one. At this time he was only twenty-one and had no experience, knowledge, friends or money to help him in the serious situation. He and Roberta sought the aid of druggists and doctors. They made a few. feeble efforts to relieve Roberta from the fast approaching disaster. All of these were futile, and, driven to madness, they watched the days and weeks lengthen into months, without knowing which way to turn. Meanwhile the affair with Sondra was growing more serious day by day, and Clyde's dream of social position and wealth, to say nothing of his desire for Sondra, was made helpless by Roberta and her impending motherhood.

One day in the midst of his dire distress he chanced to read a story in a newspaper which told of the capsizing of a canoe on a lonely lake and the drowning of a young man and woman. Neither one was found, but the boy's hat was left floating on the water. Instantly the suggestion came to Clyde that the young man had purposely upset the canoe and escaped. It flashed across his mind that this might be a way out. The idea was at first repelled with horror, but as his troubles increased the thought took deeper root and he felt that this was the only way.

Finally Clyde conceived the plan of taking Roberta to a quiet place on a northern lake for a short outing, where they could take a few days' vacation which might result in marriage. Clyde and Roberta took a canoe and went out on the lake. Of course, the plan did not work out as he expected. He somehow could not bring himself to do the deed. Still, a quarrel resulted, the boat overturned and he swam away. A few days later Roberta was found dead in the lake and Clyde's hat floating on the water. At once the coroner and detectives scented a murder case. They went to the State's Attorney; he was languishing in an obscure county seat, but even here was ambitious to be elected judge. In this tragedy he saw his chance. The young lawyer immediately took up the trail, which was not hard to follow. Hotel registers, letters, guides and many folk who had seen them together, as well as one woman on the shore of the lake who heard Roberta's cries, were easily marshaled. One or two necessary links were supplied by an ambitious detective and the case was complete. Clyde was arrested and his uncle employed a lawyer for his defense.

The trial is exceedingly well done. The result was inevitable. The story of the scion of a rich family who had ruined one girl and was in love with another who offered fine social advantages was told with all the embellishments that go with the mad man-hunt that passes as righteous indignation. Clyde was, of course, convicted and sentenced to death in the electric chair. Through it all he was befogged and dazed. Then followed the weary agony of waiting for the Supreme Court, which affirmed the verdict. After that the watching in the death cell, and the inevitable parson, who was really a kind fellow and managed to save the boy's soul at least; the long, weary journey of his poor, stricken and pathetic mother to see her son; the last hours; and his final disappearance through the fatal door to the iron chair—are told as only Dreiser could tell them.

One who knows Dreiser's work could almost see the end from the beginning. One's feelings of resentment are almost turned from Clyde to Dreiser, who, with the relentlessness of fate and the logic of life, takes Clyde step by step from the city mission to the electric chair, and Roberta from the factory to the embraces of the deep, cold waters of the lake; and still one cannot get away from the fact that it is a true story of countless victims of fate.

"An American Tragedy" is a somber, gruesome tale. It is not relieved by a single flash of color or light of joy. Dreiser carries the story straight, honest and true to the inevitable end. One thing, at least, is sure: it is deadly interesting from the beginning to the last word. One hardly stops to realize that he is gripped in the hands of a master. Such a master of technique and tragedy as the world has seldom known. One is not reading; he is living— and dying! He is held in a spell from the first page to the eight hundred and thirty-fifth. When he has finished the book it lingers and haunts and plays with his emotions as few books have ever done.

Whether this book will sell, I cannot guess. In this weary world people want to be amused. They like pleasant pictures, however fantastic or impossible they may be. They do not dare to look at life. Mr. Dreiser will not lie. He will not use his marvelous powers to trick, deceive and please.

It is useless to discuss what form art should take. This depends on the artist. The crowd will turn to Harold Bell Wright and the rest. They wish to be fed on lies. Mr. Dreiser could no doubt do this if he would. For his honesty and fidelity the world will never give him a cash return. He must know this better than any one else. "One cannot eat his cake and keep it too." Even though Mr. Dreiser may live and die poor and neglected: even though his art and work may be criticized and derided, still that part of the public which thinks and feels will understand his fanatical devotion to truth and will recognize Mr. Dreiser as one of the few real writers who has never wavered nor been afraid; and he will one day be acknowledged one of the master artists of the world.

Joseph Wood Krutch

Crime and Punishment

Mr. Dreiser's new novel is the crowning achievement of the work which he began a quarter of a century ago. To him it seemed then that novelists had lost themselves in their own refinement, that, enamored of moral delicacy and psychological subtleties, they had forgotten the simple motives by which the vast majority of mankind are moved; so with a single shrug he sloughed off once and for all the implications of the theory that man is primarily a moral animal and he did this much as the behaviorists in psychology sloughed off the soul. Let us, he said in effect, take life as I have observed it and let us see if it may not be explained upon the basis of what was afterwards called, in a brilliant analysis of his world, "a theory of animal conduct." Thus he began and thus, with a dogged insistence almost unmatched in literature, he has continued, unshaken by vituperation or neglect and unchanged by a growing fame; content to interpret an ugly world in terms of an ugly theory.

It is not, be it understood, that he denies the existence of delicate feelings or of moral restraints. The present book begins with a scene in which the family of Clyde, the hero, send up from a street corner the plaintive wail of a hymn which beats against the wall of a skyscraper and loses itself in the passing throng. Clyde himself is not unaware of the moral precepts which his parents have inculcated, nor is he unmoved by the thought of another's pain. But these things are pale shadows in comparison with needs and lusts which are nourished not by ideas and habits but by blood. They may go forth to battle but they never win; they may haunt the mind like overtones or like ghosts but they never direct a crucial action. Given a man strong enough, the lust for flesh and for power will lead him, if chance happens to favor, through the career of "The Financier"; given a man weak as the hero of "An American Tragedy" and, fortune against him, he will end with murder and the electric chair. One may revolt and rage if one likes; one may deny to Dreiser any universality for his philosophy; but one may not deny him his novels. He himself may choose what stories he wishes to tell, and no one can question either the ring of truth in the incidents or the

Reprinted from *The Nation*, CXXII (February 10, 1926), 152.

adequacy of the motives assigned. Thus and for these reasons murders are done.

Dostoevski told once and for all the story of a metaphysical murder; he showed how an idea born of logic and carried through to a logical conclusion might lead a man by a series of reasonable steps to take a life. But murderers are not ordinarily moral philosophers, and Dreiser has told with almost equal finality the story of one of those more typical murders which merely happen. He has shown a young man, neither better nor worse than thousands, led step by step into a situation from which it seems that murder alone can furnish an escape. He has shown him caught in a web of pleasant little sins committed at the behest of the common desires indulged by half mankind, and he has shown him so little plotting with deliberate malice that at the instant of the crime itself he had not yet made up his mind whether he would commit it or not. Then, relying still upon the simplest of motives, he has shown how a district attorney with his eye upon a coming election brought Clyde to trial before a jury anxious to wreak its vengeance upon a representative of the privileged class and how thus a fate-driven criminal is brought unjustly to justice. At no point in all the vast and closely woven story does any motive based upon moral, social, or religious abstractions count. Clyde may be explained without them and so, with equal completeness, may those who happened to be in the position to enforce the law against him.

Had Mr. Dreiser substituted for the indefinite "An" of his title the definite "The" he would not have been wholly unjustified, for his story implies, with all the force of a concrete example, the tragic failure of this, the most pretentiously moralistic nation of the world, to live in the main by any law but the law of the jungle. Clyde, born into a family which preached tenets of a fanatical religion and a puritanical morality, observed as no intelligent person can help observing the hopeless inapplicability of that religion and that morality to the world as he found it. He cast them off to live by the commandments which his desires dictated because they alone had, in his experience, any real authenticity; and though a little knowledge or experience of the world as it is might have saved him, no amount of conventional moral instruction or religious training could have done so. Born an animal into an animal world he went clumsily to work to win for himself the satisfactions which all about him were winning, and for his clumsiness he was punished; but the civilization in which he found himself was one which had offered him no choice save that between a feebly sentimental religion and a disastrous experiment in anarchy. He had, in a word, the misfortune to be born in a country which offers in a hundred thousand churches to teach how to renounce life but which considers it highly immoral to teach how to live.

Unfortunately there is no space in a review so brief as this must be to describe the excellences which make this novel a complete justification not only of Mr. Dreiser's theories in so far as they apply to the milieu which he has chosen but of his art as well; it must suffice to say that the story, continuously interesting and continuously terrible, marches forward with a resistless energy. Incident is piled upon incident and fact upon fact, but never—and this distinguishes the present from all the other long novels of the author—does the structure grow unwieldy or the interest falter. Nor, it must be added, do the much-advertised faults of Mr. Dreiser's style come between the reader and the events which he is following; for so absorbing are the things communicated that one forgets completely the manner in which they are communicated—a fact which must mean, I take it, that Mr. Dreiser's style is, for his own purpose, perfect. "An American Tragedy" is, in fine, the greatest of its author's works, and that can hardly mean less than that it is the greatest American novel of our generation.

H. L. Mencken

Dreiser in 840 Pages

Whatever else this vasty double-header may reveal about its author, it at least shows brilliantly that he is wholly devoid of

Reprinted from *A Mencken Chrestomathy* (New York: Alfred A. Knopf, 1926), pp. 501-5, by permission of the publisher. Copyright 1926 by Alfred A. Knopf, Inc. and renewed 1954 by H. L. Mencken. The review first appeared in somewhat different form in *The American Mercury*, VII (March 1926), 379-81.

what may be called literary tact. A more artful and ingratiating fellow, facing the situation that confronted him, would have met it with a far less difficult book. It was ten years since he had published his last novel, and all his old customers, it is reasonable to assume, were hungry for another—all his old customers and all his new customers. His publisher, after a long and gallant battle, had at last chased off the comstocks who sought to hamstring him. Rivals, springing up at intervals, had all succumbed. The Dreiser cult, once grown somewhat wobbly, was full of new strength and enthusiasm. The time was thus plainly at hand to make a ten-strike. What was needed was a book full of all the sound and solid Dreiser merits, and agreeably free from the familiar Dreiser defects—a book carefully designed and smoothly written, with no puerile clichés in it and no maudlin moralizing—in brief, a book aimed deliberately at readers of a certain taste, and competent to estimate good workmanship. Well, how did Dreiser meet the challenge? He met it, characteristically, by throwing out the present shapeless and forbidding monster—a heaping cartload of raw materials for a novel, with rubbish of all sorts intermixed—a vast, sloppy, chaotic thing of 385,000 words—at least 250,000 of them unnecessarys. Such is scientific salesmanship as Dreiser understands it. Such is his reply to a pleasant invitation to a party.

The plot is extremely simple. Clyde Griffiths, the son of a street preacher in Kansas City, revolts against the piety of his squalid home, and gets himself a job as bellboy in a gaudy hotel. There he acquires a taste for the luxuries affected by traveling salesmen, and is presently a leader in shop-girl society. An automobile accident, for which he is not to blame, forces him to withdraw discreetly, and he proceeds to Chicago, where he goes to work in a club. One day his father's rich brother, a collar magnate from Lycurgus, N. Y., is put up there by a member, and Clyde resolves to cultivate him. The old boy, taking a shine to the youngster, invites him to Lycurgus, and gives him a job in the factory. There ensues the conflict that makes the story. Clyde has hopes, but very little ready cash; he is thus forced to seek most of his recreation in low life. But as a nephew to old Samuel Griffiths he is also taken up by the Lycurgus *haut ton*. The conflict naturally assumes the form of girls. Roberta Alden, a beautiful female operative in the factory, falls in love with him and yields herself to him. Almost simultaneously Sonda Finchley, an even more beautiful society girl, falls in love with him and promises to marry him. Clyde is ambitious and decides for Sondra. But at that precise moment

Roberta tells him that their sin has found her out. His reply is to take her to a lonely lake and drown her. The crime being detected, he is arrested, put on trial, convicted, and electrocuted.

A meagre tale. Hardly more, in fact, than the plot of a three page story in *True Confessions*. But Dreiser rolls it out to such lengths that it becomes, in the end, a sort of sequence of serials. The whole first volume, of 431 pages of small type, brings us only to the lamentable event of Roberta's pregnancy. The home life of the Griffithses in Kansas City is described in detail. We make intimate acquaintance with the street preacher himself, a poor fanatic, always trusting in the God who has fooled him incessantly, and with his pathetic, drab wife, and with his daughter Esta, who runs away with a vaudeville actor and comes home with a baby. There ensues a leisurely and meticulous treatise upon the life of the bellboys in the rococo Green-Davidson Hotel—how they do their work, what they collect in tips, how they spend their evenings, what sort of girls they fancy. The automobile accident is done in the same spacious manner. Finally, we get to Lycurgus, and page after page is devoted to the operations of the Griffiths factory, and to the elegant doings in Lycurgus society, and to the first faint stirrings, the passionate high tide, and the disagreeable ebb of Clyde's affair with Roberta. So much for Volume I: 200,000 words. In Volume II we have the murder, the arrest, the trial and the execution: 185,000 more.

Obviously, there is something wrong here. Somewhere or other, there must be whole chapters that could be spared. I find, in fact, many such chapters—literally dozens of them. They incommode the action, they swamp and conceal the principal personages, and they lead the author steadily into his weakness for banal moralizing and trite, meaningless words. In "The 'Genius'" it was *trig* that rode him; in "An American Tragedy" it is *chic*. Did *chic* go out in 1896? Then so much the better! It is the mark of an unterrified craftsman to use it in 1926—more, to rub it in mercilessly. Is Freudism stale, even in Greenwich Village? Ahoy, then, let us heave in a couple of bargeloads of complexes—let us explain even judges and district attorneys in terms of suppressions. Is the "chemic" theory of sex somewhat fly-blown? Then let us trot it out, and give it a polishing with the dish-rag. Is there such a thing as sound English, graceful English, charming and beautiful English? Then let us defy a world of scoundrels, half Methodist and half esthetic, with such sentences as this one:

The "death house" in this particular prison was one of those crass erections and maintenances of human insensibility and stupidity principally for which no one primarily was really responsible.

And such as this:

Quite everything of all this was being published in the papers each day.

What is one to say of such dreadful bilge? What is one to say of a novelist who, after a quarter of a century at his trade, still writes it? What one is to say, I feel and fear, had better be engraved on the head of a pin and thrown into the ocean: there is such a thing as critical *politesse*. Here I can only remark that sentences of the kind I have quoted please me very little. One of them to a page is enough to make me very unhappy. In "An American Tragedy"—or, at all events, in parts of it—they run to much more than that. Is Dreiser actually deaf to their dreadful cacophony? I can't believe it. He can write, on occasion, with great clarity, and even with a certain grace. I point, for example, to Chapter XIII of Book III, and to the chapter following. There is here no idiotic "quite everything of all this," and no piling up of infirm adverbs. There is, instead, straightforward and lucid writing, which is caressing in itself and gets the story along. But elsewhere! . . .

Thus the defects of this gargantuan book. They are the old defects of Dreiser, and he seems to be quite unable to get rid of them. They grow more marked, indeed, as he passes into later life. His writing in "Jennie Gerhardt" was better than his writing in "The 'Genius,'" and so was his sense of form, of structure. But what of the more profound elements? What of his feeling for character, his capacity to imagine situations, his skill at reaching the emotions of the reader? I can only say that I see no falling off in this direction. "An American Tragedy," as a work of art, is a colossal botch, but as a human document it is searching and full of a solemn dignity, and at times it rises to the level of genuine tragedy. Especially the second volume. Once Roberta is killed and Clyde faces his fate, the thing begins to move, and thereafter it roars on, with ever increasing impetus, to the final terrific smash. What other American novelist could have done it? His method, true enough, is the simple, bald·one of the reporter—but of *what* a reporter! And who could have handled so magnificently the last scenes in the deathhouse? Here his very defects come to his aid. What we behold is the gradual, terrible irresistible approach of doom—the slow slipping away of hopes. The thing somehow has the effect of a tolling of bells. It is clumsy. It lacks all grace. But it is tremendously moving.

In brief, the book improves as it nears its shocking climax—a humane fact, indeed, for the reader. The first volume heaves and pitches, and the second, until the actual murder, is full of psychologizing that usually fails to come off. But once the poor girl is in the water, there is a change, and thereafter "An American Tragedy" is Dreiser at his plodding, booming best. The means are often bad, but the effects are superb. One gets the same feeling of complete reality that came from "Sister Carrie," and especially from the last days of Hurstwood. The thing ceases to be a story, and becomes a harrowing reality. Dreiser, I suppose, regards himself as an adept at the Freudian necromancy. He frequently uses its terms, and seems to take its fundamental doctrines very seriously. But he is actually a behaviorist of the most advanced wing. What interests him primarily is not what people think, but what they do. He is full of a sense of their helplessness. They are, to him, automata thrown hither and thither by fate—but suffering tragically under every buffet. Their thoughts are muddled and trivial—but they can feel. And Dreiser feels with them, and can make the reader feel with them. It takes skill of a kind that is surely not common. Good writing is far easier.

The Dreiserian ideology does not change. Such notions as he carried out of the experiences of his youth still abide with him. They take somewhat curious forms. The revolt of youth, as he sees it, is primarily a revolt against religious dogmas and forms. He is still engaged in delivering Young America from the imbecilities of a frozen Christianity. And the economic struggle, in his eye, has a bizarre symbol: the modern American hotel. Do you remember Carrie Meeber's first encounter with a hotel beefsteak in "Sister Carrie"? And Jennie Gerhardt's dumb wonder before the splendors of that hotel in which her mother scrubbed the grand staircase? There are hotels, too, and aplenty, in "The Titan" and "The 'Genius' "; toward the end of the latter there is a famous description, pages long, of the lobby of a New York apartment house, by the Waldorf-Astoria out of the Third avenue car-barn. It was a hotel that lured Jennie (like Carrie before her) to ruin, and it is a hotel that starts Clyde Griffiths on his swift journey to the chair. I suggest a more extensive examination of the matter, in the best Dreiser-Freud style. Let some ambitious young *Privat Dozent* tackle it.

So much for "An American Tragedy." Hire your pastor to read the first volume for you. But don't miss the second.

Stuart Sherman

Mr. Dreiser in Tragic Realism

What is comedy?

A selection of truths about the follies of 1925.

What is tragedy?

The whole truth about the follies of 1925. That is the subject of this book.

Many of the younger novelists in these whirling days speak of Theodore Dreiser reverently, yet retrospectively—much as free verse writers ten years ago used to speak of Whitman. Youngsters who think to shelve him with the retiring title of "the grand old man of realism" reckon without his large, stolid, literary ambition, which, to my mind, is his most salient and admirable moral characteristic. As a novelist he has been silent these ten years. Yes, but with a brooding and pregnant silence! In silence and isolation he has been industriously harvesting, like some old bear of the mountains cleaning up a great thicket of blackberries. And now with his familiar huge plantigrade tread he comes lumbering down the trail with a massive 800-page American tragedy which makes the performances of most of his rivals and successors look like capering accomplishments of rabbits and squirrels.

I shall not quarrel with any one who contends that "An American Tragedy" is the worst written great novel in the world. There are few forms of bad writing which it does not copiously illustrate. Every horror which the schoolmarm teaches the fourth-grade pupil

Reprinted from *The New York Herald Tribune*, January 3, 1926, Sec. 6, pp. 1-3; included in Stuart Sherman's *The Main Stream* (New York: Scribner's, 1927), pp. 134-44.

to avoid the "Father of Modern American Realism" riots in: "illy-dressed," "eventuate," "demeaned," in the sense of degraded; "enthused," "different to," "emasculate structure" of an anemic young girl, "via marriage," "via her determination," "the mentating section of her brain," an "ideational lake," scraps of all technical jargons, all varieties of journalese, French tags, queer coinages, and long wallflower words of Greek and Latin origin, serving purely decorative purposes.

Nor are these the most serious defects of Mr. Dreiser's style. There are chapters in which he is slower and more difficult than Proust. In dialogue and exciting narrative passages he often achieves simplicity and fair speed. But the moment he begins to "psychologize" he flounders in a morass of parenthetical and concessive clauses, slovenly beyond belief with repetitions, and infuriatingly clogged with "connective tissue"—"At the same time," "Also that despite," "And although, because of it," "And although, according to," "And in spite of the fact that"—till one is ready to yell with the torture of it.

And yet a most impressive novel. One has to take it seriously, if one takes it at all. Somehow—astonishing to relate—I feel as if this book had been very expressly left on my critical doorstep. I am not at liberty to think that Mr. Dreiser wrote it to please me. But in more than one way it does please and encourage me. It cheers me especially by demonstrating that a novelist need not stop growing at forty-four and work thenceforward on the formula which he adopted at thirty. Mr. Dreiser is taller and broader than when he wrote "The 'Genius.' " This new book marks a long stride toward a genuine and adequate realism. In order to indicate clearly the direction of his development I must briefly review his position up to 1915.

From "Sister Carrie," 1900, to "The 'Genius,' " 1915, Mr. Dreiser wrote fiction from outside American society, looking in. There were both advantages and disadvantages in that position. At his point of view, he was almost completely insensible to the force and validity of multitudinous complex powers which constantly operate within the social structure. He was incapable of understanding, for example, that etiquette has as much tensile strength as Bessemer steel. In compensation, he was able to observe the operation of other large powers of which the insiders are often unconscious, as they are of the diurnal and annual movements of the earth. He began his literary career with an overwhelming impression of what the sun, the moon, gravitation and a Cave Man ancestry were doing to him and to the captive animals inside the flimsy cage called civilization. The intensity of his vision of natural forces blotted out, for him, or reduced to insignificance, human efforts to introduce art and design among the gigantic conflicts of nature.

Born in a Mid-Western German Catholic family, Mr. Dreiser had accepted, he tells us, till he was well on in his adolescence a conventional account of society and a religious picture of the universe. Then came awakening experience with numerous girls of a sort, with numerous newspapers of a sort, politicians of a sort, captains of industry of a sort, and one thing and another—including browsing in Haeckel, Darwin, Spencer, etc. In consequence of this experience, with which he was quite unequipped to deal critically, he rushed with journalistic speed and violence to the conclusion there was nothing solid or real in this religious, legal and conventional account of the world and the societies of men. From end to end it was a romantic fiction, such as he himself was accustomed to fabricate by way of a news story for unscrupulous editors. Or it was merely a dull sham, maintained by hypocrites with smug faces and starched shirtfronts.

The real world, he concluded, after considerable introspection and reportorial looking in at the windows of several cities—the real world was composed of money-hungry and sex-hungry males and females, who, so far as the heat of their blood supported them, seized what they wanted and ran off with it, or rushed upon one another in carnal rages under the impulse of forces which they were helpless to resist—the devil taking the hindmost.

The only laws which enforced themselves in this real world were biological, physical and chemical. Accordingly, these became the only laws which commanded his respect. Whoever conformed or attempted to conform to a religious or moral "code" he was inclined to rate as a coward, a fool, or a "ragbag moralistic ass." He embraced "realism"; it offered an escape from the inferiority of a class subjugated by its morality. The successful, enviable, admirable denizens of the real world, he opined, were the Cowperwoods and the Witlas—as long as their luck lasted. The truly "virtuous," he held, were those whom nature had made strong and ruthless in the eternal struggle for the fierce pleasures and the unconscious biological ends of the animal creation.

Ten years ago, in an article subsequently included in "On Contemporary Literature," I carefully examined Mr. Dreiser's work up to and including "The 'Genius.'" It appeared to me then that he was the outstanding representative in American fiction of a point of view which I then considered, and still consider, tragic, disastrous. It was easy to show that the informing spirit of his work was naturalism rawly conceived—the crude "jungle" philosophy which I have just outlined. I thought the logical issue of such philosophy was tragedy—such tragedy as the nations of Europe were then staging in the name of "realistic" politics. It struck me that this philosophy was nowhere near so realistic as its advocates tried to make it out. It seemed to me inadequate—inadequate as a guide to civilized conduct, inadequate as an explanation of the behavior of men and women when they were civil. I suggested that a more adequate designation for it would be "barbaric naturalism."

There was, I say, no difficulty in showing the pervasive presence of it in Mr. Dreiser's novels. Up to that time he had not attempted to imitate the artful and deceptive "objectivity" and "impersonality" of the Flaubertian technique. He was a propagandist in the open, and very much bent on letting his readers know what he was driving at. His novels were elaborate documentations of a preconceived thesis. He was not pursuing truth but browbeating it into the service of a crude theory. His naïve naturalism shaped his plot and colored his characterization. But it also protruded defiantly above the surface of his narratives. It was explicit in little dissertations which a reader blind to its presence elsewhere could not fail to plump against.

In the decade since "The 'Genius,' " Mr. Dreiser has been observing, meditating and revising his views of American society, the nature of reality and the nature of realistic fiction. He has put forth several plays; two books of observation—"A Hoosier Holiday" and "The Color of a Great City"—a collection of moral ruminations in "Hey Rub-A-Dub-Dub" and a highly illuminating autobiographical work, "A Book About Myself," 1922.

This piece of autobiography is as valuable to the student of Mr. Dreiser as "A Story Teller's Story" is to the student of Mr. Anderson. It substantiates the impression which one receives from the novels. It lays before us the elementary psychological stuff out of which Mr. Dreiser had molded his heroes and his heroines as well. Comparison of the autobiography with the fiction indicates, I think, that this author has little power of penetrating antipathetic types. He specializes in the primary instincts. But he understands himself pretty well and he constructs his men and women out of parcels of himself.

In his years as a newspaper reporter, between 1890 and 1894, he developed, if we may believe him, from an unlicked bear cub, an untrained, inexperienced, formless and hungry youth, into an impecunious Don Juan, sentimental, inflammable, vain and greedy for the luxuries which insulted his poverty—in the street, in the hotel lobby, in the ornate barroom; the flash of studs and stickpins, the rustle of silk, the shine of patent leather shoes, the distinction of tailor-made coats, the glitter of glass and the rich harmony of potted palms and mahogany.

In "An American Tragedy" Mr. Dreiser presents the life history of much such another youth—a youth, however, who never got past the passion for girls and stickpins to the larger and more engrossing passion for understanding how he came to be what he was, and why he did what he did.

I think this story must have originated in the "tragedy" itself. I conceive that Mr. Dreiser began with the tragic fact and worked backward, with no thesis whatever, with no ulterior purpose beyond the complete uncovering of all the intricate network of causes which led to the event.

Mr. Dreiser has either renounced or effectually suppressed the naïve naturalism of his previous novels. There are no interspersed philosophical dissertations here. There is no special pleading, no coloring of the news, no studied continuous aspersion of the customs and habits of men in civil or religious societies from the untenable point of view of "barbaric naturalism."

No; Mr. Dreiser has changed both his method and his point of view. He has withdrawn to a position of far more complete artistic "detachment." He gives me now for the first time an impression of "impersonality," "objectivity," "impartiality." He appears to me now for the first time in his fiction to be seeking sincerely and pretty successfully to tell the truth, all the relevant truth and nothing but the truth—and with such proportion and emphasis that every interest involved shall feel itself adequately represented.

Clyde Griffiths is the "hero." He is the son of itinerant evangelists who sing and march and pray in the streets of Kansas City. Clyde is ashamed of his parents, of their piety, and their poverty, and of the dreariness of life in the Bethel Independent Mission where they dwell. They have exchanged animality for hymn books and a spirituality so thin that it is a dubious bargain. Christian nurture has not sunk in. Enviously he looks upon the advantages enjoyed by unconsecrated society: "Oh, the fine clothes, the handsome houses, the watches, rings, pins, that some boys sported; the dandies many youths of his years already were! Some parents of boys of his years actually gave them cars of their own to ride in. They were to be seen upon the principal streets of Kansas City flitting to and fro like flies. And pretty girls with them. And he had nothing. And he never had had."

Clyde gets a job, first as a soda fountain clerk in a drug store, and then as a bellboy in the Green-Davidson Hotel. The first book of this novel, running to 148 pages, might be called "A Bellboy's Romance"; and there Mr. Dreiser skirts one of the greatest possibilities of fiction: the corruption of the lower classes by the upper classes. Clyde is a selfish, vain, greedy little beast, and quickly learns to lie to his mother about his wages, to dress with some "elegance," to drink, to feast and to play with girls of about his sort. His sister "gets into trouble." His mother comes to him for pecuniary help. He wants his money to buy his girl a fur coat. But, becoming involved in a serious and disgraceful automobile accident, he evades all his problems by running away from them. The whelp is selfish and a coward to the marrow of his bones.

After an interim of wandering and of rehabilitation as a bellboy in the Union League Club of Chicago Clyde makes a fresh start in the cotton mills of a prosperous uncle in Lycurgus, New York. Here his ignorant amorousness soon gets him deeply involved with a hitherto respectable girl employed in his department. If you will compare Mr. Dreiser's romantic glozing of Jennie Gerhardt's predicament with his exhaustive and astoundingly intelligent study of the shame and misery and torment of Roberta Alden in being pregnant, penniless, without a husband, and dependent on a resourceless sneak, you will readily recognize that Mr. Dreiser's ability to see all the elements in a situation has grown enormously since he published that earlier sentimental tale.

While surreptitiously carrying on this affair Clyde's snobbishness and his lust for luxurious living lead to an attachment in the "higher circles" of Lycurgus society. Mr. Dreiser's women generally have no individuality beyond their physique, their softness, and their clothes. If he has met with a feminine intelligence, he has made no boast of the encounter. This girl of the upper circles, Sondra, has impressed me mainly, as she did Clyde, by a tailored suit which followed her form exactly and which was enhanced by a small dark leather hat, pulled fetchingly low over her eyes. In addition, there was a leather "belt" of the same color around her neck. Note also that by a leather leash she led a French bull. To

Clyde, "youth and beauty in such a station as this represented the ultimate triumph of the female." I have forgotten to mention that in her more tender moments this leather-panoplied creature called her lover "Clydie Mydie," and so on.

Well, Clyde has $25 a week and a girl who is about to become a mother; and he is attempting to maintain social relations with the sons and daughters of the mill owners. *That* in a sense is his tragedy, and Mr. Dreiser most impressively lays it bare. But out of Clyde's economic and moral predicament a death results, for which he is held criminally responsible, though perhaps he is technically innocent, yet not without murderous malice aforethought.

There is a pretty situation for dramatic treatment. Mr. Dreiser makes the most of it. His exhibition of the antecedent and attendant circumstances is complete and convincing. So is his analysis of the psychology of Clyde and the working girl. It is of a masterly exhaustiveness. The reader is put in possession of everything relevant. Then through the greater part of the second volume we attend a long drawn-out trial, in the course of which we hear everything that public opinion and the law can say for and against Clyde. Then we get the verdict of the boy's mother and of his latest sweetheart and of the court of appeals and of the Governor of the state and of a sympathetic, intelligent and conscientious clergyman, and finally of Clyde himself. The law, the gospel, and the individual conscience all have a fair hearing. For Mr. Dreiser, sternly detached, lets every fact and opinion speak for itself.

I have not the slightest intention of offending the author by suggesting that he has become a sound moralist. I imagine that is quite unintentional. All that he has sought is comprehensive veracity. But only this morning I assured a young woman that if she would read Mr. Dreiser's latest novel it would permanently deter her from folly. I showed her the book. "Yes," she replied with an appraising glance at the two volumes, "but by that time it would be too late."

In its larger features the construction of "An American Tragedy" is as solid as a bank building. It is very long, to be sure, but there is little in it which is not functional, not a part of Mr. Dreiser's ponderous design. I was very nervous for fear the roof would fall during a couple of sagging chapters early in the second volume; but, no, he slowly swung his heavy timbers into place, restored his tension and maintained it to the end. The structure of a novel he has mastered. It is the structure of the sentence which remains a mystery to him. Often he plunges into a sentence head foremost, "trusting to God Almighty to get him out of it"; and is vouchsafed no divine aid. And yet the work as a whole is massively impressive. I do not know where else in American fiction one can find the situation here presented dealt with so fearlessly, so intelligently, so exhaustively, so veraciously, and *therefore* with such unexceptionable moral effect.

2. Studies

Frederick J. Hoffman

The Scene of Violence: Dostoevsky and Dreiser

The surface similarities of *Crime and Punishment* and Dreiser's *An American Tragedy* are many, and they may help to document the radical changes in the literature of violence since Dostoevsky's time. It is necessary to point up the similarities of landscape. Dreiser's principal figures are social, in the sense that he allows scenes to image forth the inconsistencies of the human will. In fact, his most effective formal devices are these contrasts of scene; they provide a scenic grammar of the novel. Like Dostoevsky, Dreiser is anxious to explore the extent to which the will of man has isolated itself from spiritual sanctions. The Dreiser hero wishes rather than wills, but insofar as his wishes project into the world of objects they create or help to make possible elaborate Aladdin displays of vulgar luxuries. One such display is the lobby of the Green-Davidson Hotel, in Kansas City.

> [Clyde Griffiths] went direct to a green-marbled doorway which opened from the rear of this drug-store into the lobby of the hotel. Once through it, he beheld a lobby, the like of which, for all his years but because of the timorous poverty that had restrained him from exploring such a world, was more arresting, quite, than anything he had seen before. It was all so lavish. Under his feet was a checkered black-and-white marble floor. Above him a coppered and stained and gilded ceiling. And supporting this, a veritable forest of black marble columns as highly polished as the floor— glassy smooth. And between the columns . . . were lamps, statuary, rugs, palms, chairs, divans, tête-à-têtes—a prodigal display.

This assortment of property effects, designed as Dreiser says to give the masses a feeling of luxury, acts immediately to soften Clyde's will. He is at the moment an observer of the scene. Ultimately he will become its victim. The scenes of the ensuing pages contrast vividly with the nightmarish disarray of Raskolnikov's culminating hallucination. As bellhop in the Green-Davidson

Reprinted from *Modern Fiction Studies*, VI (Summer 1960), 100-105, by permission. *Modern Fiction Studies*, © 1960, by Purdue Research Foundation, Lafayette, Indiana.

Hotel, Clyde is privileged to look into one after another of the most casual of human indulgences. He is throughout a passive servant, even of the least ingratiating of these pleasures. The bellhop's uniform stamps him as a flunkey. He never decisively initiates either pleasure or crime. Nor can he be said to be in any sense a "meditative man." He is overawed by the hotel, bored and embarrassed by his family (who wander the streets as evangelists), resentful of his status, surprised into gratitude for the notice of his betters, and eventually invited passively to withdraw from the crime his victim has all but suicidally collaborated with him in committing.

Perhaps the most vivid of contrasts can be seen in Clyde's first walk along the streets of Lycurgus' privileged upperclass area.

> He found himself ambling on and on until suddenly he was out of the business district again and in touch with a wide and tree-shaded thoroughfare of residences, the houses of which, each and every one, appeared to possess more room space, lawn space, general ease and repose and dignity even than any with which he had ever been in contact. . . . So many imposing wrought-iron fences, flower-bordered walks, grouped trees and bushes, expensive and handsome automobiles either beneath porte-cochères within or speeding along the broad thoroughfares without.

The truth of this landscape that Clyde never really discovers is its unreality. It is a deliberately placid, smoothly peaceful but non-existent world. It lies at one pole of the two unrealities Clyde endures. The other is the grim and dismal street-world where his mother and father attempt to preach the word of God.

The two extremes are in effect the principal patterns of scene in the landscape which will eventually lead to Clyde's death. Remembering the "easy life" of the Green-Davidson Hotel, he wishes somehow to make it his permanent privilege. When the opportunity does come, he is already involved with a daughter of the depressed classes. Roberta Alden is, in terms of any effective comparison with *Crime and Punishment*, the counterpart of the pawnbroker whom Raskolnikov murders. In the one case she is "in the way"; in the other, she is a "first step," whose death is the one evil a superior man is permitted that he may perform a thousand good acts. Miss Alden, pregnant and adamantly insistent upon marriage, is on the way to destroying Clyde's prospects of reaching that easy, quiet, and inaccessible world he had seen in his first days in Lycurgus.

At this point *An American Tragedy* becomes abjectly itself, bows before the necessities of the naturalist disposition toward violence. Naturalism begins by saying that the universe has a specific character and as such is indifferent to the will of man— not that it is hostile, but that it is simply indifferent. Clyde Griffiths does not will the destruction of Roberta; he merely wishes it, and she obliges him. The affair presents almost no hard core of specificity to contemplate, and the speculations over Clyde's "crime" are therefore innately ambiguous. The ambiguities do not result from any violent struggle of the hero to define his meaning to himself, but instead are a consequence of the act's not being in any way firm enough to submit to probing.

This maze of uncertainty is vividly revealed in Dreiser's style, at the crucial moment of his attempt to sum up Clyde. He has brought Roberta all the way to a deserted lake in upstate New York, on the pretense of their having a pre-marital honeymoon. He had begun by vaguely planning a crime, but the force of will needed did not initially exist and he is merely imitating a suggestion the world outside had offered him. When the awful moment arrives, he suffers the agonies of a willess will in a position where action is both indispensable and impossible.

> At this cataclysmic moment, and in the face of the utmost, the most urgent need of action, a sudden palsy of the will—of courage —of hate or rage sufficient; and with Roberta from her seat in the stern of the boat gazing at his troubled and then suddenly distorted and fulgurous, yet weak and even unbalanced face—a face of a sudden, instead of angry, ferocious, demoniac—confused and all but meaningless in its registration of a balanced combat between fear (a chemic revulsion against death or murderous brutality that would bring death) and a harried and restless and yet self-repressed desire to do—to do—yet temporarily unbreakable here and now—a static between a powerful compulsion to do and yet not to do.

The very language chokes itself off. It is a rhetorical imitation of a state of absolute indecision. Since Clyde suffers this state, the death of Roberta cannot really be explained. Was it an act of "moral cowardice," or was there "some anger in the blow"? The novel, in its entirety but particularly in this its crucial scene, suggests a few comments on the history of force in modern literature. The force manipulated by Julien Sorel (*The Red and The Black*) in his own interests exists within range of his sensibility and will, and he is capable of acting decisively to avail himself of it. But already much of the force is in the hands of the peasantry and the townspeople, who have made of it a form of calculation and exchange. Business principles and "deals" occupy an astonishing percentage of the space in nineteenth-century novels—to the extent that there is almost nothing of any consequence left outside them. The revulsion against commercial uses of force takes the form either of extending the range of the language to a point so remote from reality that it no longer suffices to identify its enemy, or of describing the pathos, filth, disorder, and calamity of its effect upon the landscape. The objects selected to enforce this grim portraiture are arranged in a sordid light or in a semi-surrealistic disarray. Since naturalism is, in literary terms at any rate, an extension of realism, the naturalist landscape incorporates not only the sordid detail used for a very much more complex purpose by Baudelaire, Eliot, and their contemporaries, but the scene itself in which social disparities can easily be imaged. Dreiser's concern with cities, hotels, clothes, and interiors helps to identify this landscape as a social record of moral deficiencies. But the landscape does not record merely despair over the disabilities of the modern world; it is asked as well to express externally the inner dispositions of its heroes.

The *milieu* all but swallows and destroys the hero. Clyde moves from one scene to another; every event of his life is determined by its locale. If there is any complication of will in Clyde's life, it is represented by a suddenly visualized contrast of scenes: as when Clyde, in the company of his newly found wealthy friends, accidentally comes upon the dilapidated farmhouse of Roberta's parents: ". . . the mere identification of this lorn, dilapidated realm with Roberta and hence himself, was sufficient to cause him to wish to turn and run." There is no real chance of differentiation in circumstances of this sort.

When the death of Roberta is traced to Clyde and the trial begins, the scene shifts from one pole to the other. The upper class all but disappears; Sondra Finchley is referred to as a "Miss X" during the trial; Clyde is forced to stand before a jury and a courtroom audience made up entirely of Roberta's class of people. The visionary, unreal character of the Lycurgus landscape, which Clyde had observed when he first walked there, is confirmed in its disappearance. From this time forward the dregs of Kansas City and the factory district of Lycurgus take over. This is not a balanced representation of Clyde's worlds at all. He is doomed to die without any real exploration in depths of the terms of his having been victimized. The Reverend Duncan Macmillan strives mightily to bring him to God before he dies; but God is the streets of Kansas City, and the Alden farmhouse, and while Macmillan might bring Clyde to some kind of psychological insight into his role in Roberta's death, he cannot effectively make him accept the religious definition of the act.

The tragedy of Dreiser's hero is singularly weak in the matter of effectively ranging his will against the scene. He is taken for a long ride, but he is never at the wheel. This absence of willed participation in his hero's role makes Clyde so exclusively the victim as to bring seriously into quesion his meriting any role at all. There is no way in which the several scenes of *An American Tragedy* may be said to define a pattern of assailant-victim relationship. If we say that Clyde is entirely victim, we are faced with the question, victim of what? Raskolnikov participates actively in both crime and punishment; he not only wills the crime but goes more than halfway to accept Porfiry's invitation to confess it. Clyde does neither of these things. He is at every turn of event a passive observer of the scenes in which the terms of his crime and his punishment are being agreed upon.

Yet, in a very real sense *An American Tragedy* comes closer than *Crime and Punishment* to expressing the terms of the assailant as landscape in the modern literature of violence. Whatever the aberations of metaphysics which led Dreiser to his concept of victimization, he presents in Clyde Griffiths a victim almost totally bound to the circumstances of the controlling scenes. Clyde does not provide on his own initiative any means of understanding this situation; nor does he actively or entirely accept any explanation offered by anyone else. He is in neither sense an effective modern hero, but only a form of illustration of one stage on the way to modern heroism.

There is a crucial passage in E. A. Robinson's long meditative poem "The Man Against the Sky," in which—after he has outlined five ways in which man might go to his death—he asks the question that all naturalists must and do ask, of themselves and of their creatures:

> Are we no greater than the noise we make
> Along one blind atomic pilgrimage
> Whereon by crass chance billeted we go
> Because our brains and bones and cartilage

Will have it so?
If this we say, then let us all be still
About our share in it, and live and die
More quietly thereby.

Why not make an end of life, Robinson asks, if there is no more than death in view:

If after all that we have lived and thought,
All comes to Nought,—
If there be nothing after Now,
And we be nothing anyhow,
And we know that—why life?

The proper answer is that we do live, and that for most of us the urge to stay alive is sufficient to account for our doing so. This sentiment suggests another stage in the history of the hero's role in a literary landscape. Man lives in the security of immortality, or he is bound by an inner drive to raise his condition of life to an acceptable moral level. If the circumstances of living are not intolerable, he will merely live because he does. If, as is the case of Clyde Griffiths, he lives and acts because he sees a more attractive way of living than he presently enjoys, he will passively submit to events leading inevitably to violence and death.

There are suggestions in *An American Tragedy* of intolerable scenes; they are intolerable only because others are more attractive, but they are so intolerable that Clyde will not prevent a crime from happening in order to accept them and abide by them. This is certainly a very mild example of the assailant as landscape. The wars themselves provided more shocking and unendurable occasions. The landscape becomes an assailant when it forces the hero in literature into the role of victim. There are examples in modern literature of its forcing the individual to destroy in himself all vestiges of will, to become a victim collaborating in the crime that is his own death. Neither this extreme nor the spectacle of a hero's death like that of Noah Ackerman (Shaw's *The Young Lions*) can properly be called a culmination of the literature of violence. But the way to an understanding of it is opened when we are presented with a hero who understands neither what is being done to him, nor why he is doing it.

An American Tragedy

Do I exaggerate in saying that Theodore Dreiser has dropped out of the awareness of cultivated Americans? If so, it is but a slight exaggeration. Few young writers now model themselves on his career, and not many readers think of him as one of those literary figures whose word can transform the quality of their experience. Dreiser has suffered the fate that often besets writers caught up in cultural dispute: their work comes to seem inseparable from what has been said about it, their passion gets frozen into history.

Mention Dreiser to a bright student of literature, mention him to a literate older person, and only seldom will the response be a swift turning of memory to novels that have brought pleasure and illumination. Far more likely is a series of fixed associations: to a cragged, brooding, bearlike figure who dragged himself out of nineteenth-century poverty and provincialism, and in *Sister Carrie* composed a pioneering novel of sexual candor; or to a vague notion that the author of *The Financier* and *The Titan* turned out quantities of ill-tuned and turgid social documentation; or to a prepared judgment against a writer taken to be sluggish in thought and language, sluggishly accumulating data of destruction and failure, but deaf to the refinements of consciousness, dull to the play of sensibility, and drab, utterly and hopelessly drab in the quality of his mind.

The decline of Dreiser's reputation has not been an isolated event. It has occurred in the context, and surely as a consequence, of the counterrevolution in American culture during the past few decades. For readers educated in these years, Dreiser often became a symbol of everything a superior intelligence was supposed to avoid. For the New Critics, to whom the very possibility of a social novel seemed disagreeable; for literary students trained in the fine but narrow school of the Jamesian sensibility; for liberals easing into a modest gentility and inclined to replace a belief in social commitment with a search for personal distinction; for intellectuals delighted with the values of ambiguity, irony, complexity and impatient with the pieties of radicalism—for all such persons Dreiser became an object of disdain. He stood for an earlier age of scientism, materialism, agnosticism: all of which were now seen as hostile to the claims of moral freedom and responsibility. He represented the boorishness of the populist mentality, as it declined into anti-Semitism or veered toward a peculiarly thoughtless brand of communism. He could not think: he could only fumble with the names of ideas. He could not write: he could only pile words on top of each other. He cared not for art as such, but only for the novel as a vehicle of social and "philosophical" ideas. He was uneducated, insensitive—the novelist as mastodon.

So the indictment went, frequently right in its details, and when coming from so temperate a critic as Lionel Trilling often persuasive in result. If a few literary men, like the novelist James T. Farrell and the critic Alfred Kazin, continued to praise Dreiser as a writer of massive and poignant effects, if they insisted that attention be paid to the novels he wrote rather than to his foolish public declamations, they were not much heeded in the last few decades.

But now, when Dreiser's prejudices have begun to be forgotten and all that remains—all that need remain—are his three or four major novels, it is time for reconsideration. The early praise these books received may have been undiscriminating: we are not obliged to repeat it. Dreiser's role in assaulting the taboos of gentility can no longer excite us as once it did his admirers. And as for his faults, no great critical insight is required to identify them, since they glare out of every chapter, especially his solemnities as a cosmic voice and his habit of crushing the English language beneath a leaden embrace. Yet these faults are interwoven with large creative powers, and it can be argued that for the powers to be released there had first to be the triggering presence of the faults. Let me cite an example.

As a philosopher Dreiser can often be tiresome; yet his very lust for metaphysics, his stubborn insistence upon learning "what it's all about," helped to deepen the emotional resources from which he drew as a novelist. For he came to feel that our existence demands from us an endless contemplativeness, even if—perhaps because—we cannot think through our problems or solve our mysteries. In the frustrations he encountered when trying to extract some conceptual order from the confusion and trouble of existence, he grew more closely involved, more *at one*, with the characters he created, also confused and troubled. Somewhat like Thomas Hardy, he learned to stand back a little from the human spectacle and watch the endlessly repeated sequence of desire, effort and disintegration; and from this distance—perhaps the sole reward of his philosophical gropings—he gained a sense of the shared helplessness of men, he learned how brutal and irrelevent the impulse to moral judgment can become, and he arrived at his profoundly inclusive compassion for the whole of human life.

In the first task of the novelist, which is to create an imaginary social landscape both credible and significant, Dreiser ranks among the American giants, the very few American giants we have had. Reading *An American Tragedy* once again, after a lapse of more than twenty years, I have found myself greatly moved and shaken by its repeated onslaughts of narrative, its profound immersion in human suffering, its dredging up of those shapeless desires which lie, as if in fever, just below the plane of consciousness. How much more vibrant and tender this book is than the usual accounts of it in recent criticism might lead one to suppose! It is a masterpiece, nothing less.

II

Dreiser published *An American Tragedy* in 1925. By then he was fifty-four years old, an established writer with his own fixed and hard-won ways, who had written three first-rate novels: *Sister Carrie, Jennie Gerhardt* and *The Financier*. These books are crowded with exact observation—observation worked closely into the grain of narrative—about the customs and class structure of American society in the phase of early finance capitalism. No other novelist has absorbed into his work as much knowledge as Dreiser had about American institutions: the mechanisms of business, the stifling rhythms of the factory, the inner hierarchy of a large hotel, the chicaneries of city politics, the status arrangements of rulers and ruled. For the most part Dreiser's characters are defined through their relationships to these institutions. They writhe and suffer to win a foothold in the slippery social world or to break out of the limits of established social norms. They exhaust themselves to gain success, they destroy themselves in acts of impulsive deviancy. But whatever their individual lot, they all act out the drama of determinism—which, in Dreiser's handling, is not at all the sort of listless fatality that hostile critics would make it seem, but is rather a fierce struggle by human beings to discover the harsh limits of what is possible to them and thereby perhaps to enlarge those limits by an inch or two. That mostly they fail is Dreiser's tribute to reality.

This controlling pattern in Dreiser's novels has been well described by Bernard Rosenberg, a sociologist with a literary eye:

> Emile Durkheim had suggested in Dreiser's day that when men speak of a force external to themselves which they are powerless to control, their subject is not God but social organization. This is also Dreiser's theme, and to it he brings a sense of religious awe and wonder. "So well defined," he writes, "is the sphere of social activity, that he who departs from it is doomed" . . . Durkheim identified social facts, i.e., the existence of norms, precisely as Dreiser did: by asking what would happen if they were violated. . . . Norms develop outside the individual consciousness and exist prior to it; we internalize them and are fully aware of their grip only when our behavior is deviant. Durkheim illustrated this proposition in a dozen different ways, and so did Dreiser.

In Dreiser's early novels most of the central characters are harried by a desire for personal affirmation, a desire they can neither articulate nor suppress. They suffer from a need that their lives assume the dignity of dramatic form, and they suffer terribly, not so much because they cannot satisfy this need, but because they do not really understand it. Money, worldly success, sensual gratification, are the only ends they know or can name, but none of these slakes their restlessness. They grapple desperately for money, they lacerate themselves climbing to success, yet they remain sullen and bewildered, always hopeful for some unexpected sign by which to release their bitter craving for a state of grace or, at least, illumination. Dreiser's characters are romantics who behave as if the Absolute can be found, immaculately preserved, at the very summit of material power. Great energies can flow from this ingrained American delusion, both for the discharge of ambition and the aggressiveness of ego. And Dreiser too, because he had in his own experience shared these values and struggled, with varying effectiveness, to burn them out of his system—Dreiser too lived out, with an intense dramatic complicity, the longings and turmoil of his characters.

Yet there is usually present in his early novels a governing intelligence more copious and flexible than that of the characters. This governing intelligence is seldom revealed through direct statement, either by characters or author. So thoroughly does Dreiser recognize the bond of vulnerability between a Carrie and himself, he never moralizes. So patiently does he join a Cowperwood and a Jennie through the course of their experience, he never condescends. Taking upon himself the perils and sharing in the miseries of his characters, he leaves the privilege of admonition to others. Yet there is never really a question as to what his novels "mean," nor any serious possibility that the characters will usurp control. Through the logic of the narrative, the working-out of its implications, we are enabled to grasp with an almost visceral intensity how shallow are the standards by which the characters live.

In these early novels society figures largely as a jungle; and with good reason—the capitalism of the early twentieth century closely resembled a jungle. The characters may begin with a hard struggle for survival, but far more quickly than most of Dreiser's critics allow, they leave it behind them. Having emerged from the blunt innocence of their beginnings, they are now cursed with a fractional awareness. They can find neither peace nor fulfillment. In their half-articulate way, Dreiser's characters are beset by the same yearnings that trouble the characters of Fitzgerald and many other American novelists: a need for some principle of value by which to overcome the meanness, the littleness of their lives. To know, however, that the goals to which one has pledged one's years are trivial, yet not to know in what their triviality consists —this is a form of suffering which overcomes Dreiser's characters again and again. In all its dumb misery, it is the price, or reward, of their slow crawl to awareness. One sometimes feels that in the novels of Dreiser there is being reenacted the whole progression of the race toward the idea of the human.

The prose in these early novels is often as wretched as unsympathetic critics have said. Dreiser had little feeling for the sentence as a rhythmic unit (though he had a strong intuitive grasp of the underlying rhythm of narrative as a system of controlled variation and incremental development). He had a poor ear for the inflections of common speech, or even for the colloquial play of language. And worst of all, he had a weakness, all too common among the semieducated, for "elegant" diction and antique rhetoric. Yet, despite the many patches of gray and the occasional patches of purple prose,* Dreiser manages to accumulate large masses of

---

* "The function of language is much more largely referential in the novel than in other literary forms . . . the genre itself works by exhaustive presentation rather than by elegant concentration. This fact would no doubt explain . . . why the novel is the most translatable of genres; why many undoubtedly great novelists, from Richardson and Balzac to Hardy and Dostoevsky, often write gracelessly, and sometimes with downright vulgarity . . ."—Ian Watt, *The Rise of the Novel.*

narrative tension; he pulls one, muttering and bruised, into the arena of his imagination; and finally one has no recourse but surrender to its plenitude, its coarse and encompassing reality.

Not even Dreiser's philosophical excursions—bringing together nativist American prejudice with the very latest ideas of 1900—can break the thrust of these narratives. Dreiser's thought has by now been analyzed, mauled, and ridiculed: his distortion of social life through metaphors of brute nature, his reduction of human motive to the malignant pressure of "chemisms," his toying with notions about "the superman" in the Cowperwood novels. But it hardly matters. One brushes all this aside, resigned to the malice of a fate that could yoke together such intellectual debris with so much creative power. One brushes aside, and reads on.

III

Though surely Dreiser's major achievement, *An American Tragedy* is not the work of a master who, at the approach of old age, decides upon a revolutionary break from the premises and patterns of his earlier writing. For that order of boldness Dreiser lacked a sufficient self-awareness and sophistication as an artist; he was cut off from too much of the tradition of Western, even of American, culture to do anything but continue with his version of naturalism. He was the kind of writer who must keep circling about the point of his beginnings, forever stirred by memories of his early struggles and preoccupations. All such a writer can hope for—a very great deal—is to mine his talent to its very depth; and that Dreiser did in *An American Tragedy*. Still, there are some changes from the earlier novels, and most of them to the good.

The prose, while quite as clotted and ungainly as in the past, is now more consistent in tone and less adorned with "literary" paste gems. Solecisms, pretentiousness, and gaucherie remain, but the prose has at least the negative virtue of calling less attention to itself than in some of the earlier books. And there are long sections packed with the kind of specification that in Dreiser makes for a happy self-forgetfulness, thereby justifying Philip Rahv's remark that one finds here "a prosiness so primary in texture that if taken in bulk it affects us as a kind of poetry of the commonplace and ill-favored."

For the first and last time Dreiser is wholly in the grip of his vision of things, so that he feels little need for the buttress of comment or the decoration of philosophizing. Dreiser is hardly the writer whose name would immediately occur to one in connection

with T. S. Eliot's famous epigram that Henry James had a mind so
fine it could not be violated by ideas; yet if there is one Dreiser
novel concerning which something like Eliot's remark might apply,
it is *An American Tragedy*. What Eliot said has sometimes been
taken, quite absurdly, as if it were a recommendation for writers
to keep themselves innocent of ideas; actually he was trying to
suggest the way a novelist can be affected by ideas yet must not
allow his work to become a mere illustration for them. And of all
Dreiser's novels *An American Tragedy* is the one that seems least
cluttered with unassimilated formulas and preconceptions.

Where the earlier novels dealt with somewhat limited aspects of
American life, *An American Tragedy*, enormous in scope and ambition, requires to be judged not merely as an extended study of the
American lower middle class during the first years of the twentieth
century but also as a kind of parable of our national experience.
Strip the story to its bare outline, and see how much of American
desire it involves: an obscure youth, amiable but weak, is lifted by
chance from poverty to the possibility of winning pleasure and
wealth. To gain these ends he must abandon the pieties of his
fundamentalist upbringing and sacrifice the tender young woman
who has given him a taste of pure affection. All of society conspires
to persuade him that his goals are admirable, perhaps even sacred;
he notices that others, no better endowed than himself, enjoy the
privileges of money as if it were in the very nature of things that
they should; but the entanglements of his past now form a barrier
to realizing his desires, and to break through this barrier he
must resort to criminal means. As it happens, he does not commit
the murder he had planned, but he might as well have, for he is
trapped in the machinery of social punishment and destroyed. "So
well defined is the sphere of social activity that he who departs
from it is doomed."

Now this story depends upon one of the most deeply grounded
fables in our culture. Clyde Griffiths, the figure in Dreiser's novel
who acts it out, is not in any traditional sense either heroic or
tragic. He has almost no assertive will, he lacks any large compelling idea, he reveals no special gift for the endurance of pain.
In his puny self he is little more than a clouded reflection of the
puny world about him. His significance lies in the fact that he
represents not our potential greatness but our collective smallness,
the common denominator of our foolish tastes and tawdry ambi-
tions. He is that part of ourselves in which we take no pride, but
know to be a settled resident. And we cannot dismiss him as a

special case or an extreme instance, for his weakness is the essential shoddiness of mortality. By a twist of circumstance he could be a junior executive, a country-club favorite; he almost does manage to remake himself to the cut of his fantasy; and he finds in his rich and arrogant cousin Gilbert an exasperating double, the young man he too might be. Clyde embodies the nothingness at the heart of our scheme of things, the nothingness of our social aspirations. If Flaubert could say, *Emma Bovary, c'est moi,* Dreiser could echo, *Clyde Griffiths, he is us.*

We have then in Clyde a powerful representation of our unacknowledged values, powerful especially since Dreiser keeps a majestic balance between sympathy and criticism. He sees Clyde as a characteristic reflex of "the vast skepticism and apathy of life," as a characteristic instance of the futility of misplaced desire in a society that offers little ennobling sense of human potentiality. Yet he nevertheless manages to make the consequences of Clyde's mediocrity, if not the mediocrity itself, seem tragic. For in this youth there is concentrated the tragedy of human waste: energies, talents, affections all unused—and at least in our time the idea of human waste comprises an essential meaning of tragedy. It is an idea to which Dreiser kept returning both in his fiction and his essays:

> When one was dead one was dead for all time. Hence the reason for the heartbreak over failure here and now; the awful tragedy of a love lost, a youth never properly enjoyed. Think of living and yet not living in so thrashing a world as this, the best of one's hours passing unused or not properly used. Think of seeing this tinkling phantasmagoria of pain and pleasure, beauty and all its sweets, go by, and yet being compelled to be a bystander, a mere onlooker, enhungered and never satisfied.

The first half of *An American Tragedy* is given to the difficult yet, for Dreiser's purpose, essential task of persuading us that Clyde Griffiths, through his very lack of distinction, represents a major possibility in American experience. Toward this end Dreiser must accumulate a large sum of substantiating detail. He must show Clyde growing up in a family both materially and spiritually impoverished. He must show Clyde reaching out for the small pleasures, the trifles of desire, and learning from his environment how splendid are these induced wants. He must show Clyde, step by step, making his initiation into the world of sanctioned America, first through shabby and then luxury hotels, where he picks up the signals of status and sin. He must show Clyde as the very image and prisoner of our culture, hungering with its hungers, empty with its emptiness.

Yet all the while Dreiser is also preparing to lift Clyde's story from this mere typicality, for he wishes to go beyond the mania for the average which is a bane of naturalism. Everything in this story is ordinary, not least of all the hope of prosperity through marriage—everything but the fact that Clyde begins to act out, or is treated as if he had acted out, the commonplace fantasy of violently disposing of a used-up lover. This is the sole important departure from ordinary verisimilitude in the entire novel, and Dreiser must surely have known that it was. In the particular case upon which he drew for *An American Tragedy*, the young man did kill his pregnant girl; but Dreiser must nevertheless have realized that in the vast majority of such crises the young man dreams of killing and ends by marrying. Dreiser understood, however, that in fiction the effort to represent common experience requires, at one or two crucial points, an effect of heightening, an intense exaggeration. Clyde's situation may be representative, but his conduct must be extreme. And is that not one way of establishing the dramatic: to drive a representative situation to its limits of possibility?

In *An American Tragedy* Dreiser solved the problem which vexes all naturalistic novelists: how to relate harmoniously a large panorama of realism with a sharply contoured form. Dreiser is endlessly faithful to common experience. No one, not even the critics who have most harshly attacked the novel, would care to deny the credibility of Clyde and Roberta Alden, the girl he betrays; most of the attacks on Dreiser contain a mute testimony to his achievement, for in order to complain about his view of life they begin by taking for granted the "reality" of his imagined world. Yet for all its packed detail, the novel is economically structured—though one must understand that the criterion of economy for this kind of novel is radically different from that for a James or Conrad novel. In saying all that I do not mean anything so improbable as the claim that whatever is in the book belongs because it is there; certain sections, especially those which prepare for Clyde's trial, could be cut to advantage; but the overall architecture has a rough and impressive craftsmanship.

The action of the novel moves like a series of waves, each surging forward to a peak of tension and then receding into quietness, and each, after the first one, reenacting in a more complex and perilous fashion the material of its predecessor. Clyde in Kansas City, Clyde in Chicago, Clyde alone with Roberta in Lycurgus, Clyde on the edge of the wealthy set in Lycurgus—these divisions form the novel until the point where Roberta is drowned, and each of them acts as a reflector on the others, so that there is a mounting series of anticipations and variations upon the central theme. Clyde's early flirtation with a Kansas City shopgirl anticipates, in its chill manipulativeness, the later and more important relationship with Sondra Finchley, the rich girl who seems to him the very emblem of his fantasy. Clyde's childhood of city poverty is paralleled by the fine section presenting the poverty of Roberta's farm family. The seduction and desertion of Clyde's unmarried sister anticipates Clyde's seduction and desertion of Roberta. Clyde receives his preliminary education in the hotels where he works as bellboy, and each of these serves as a microcosm of the social world he will later break into. Clyde's first tenderness with Roberta occurs as they float on a rowboat; the near-murder, equally passive, also on a rowboat. The grasping Clyde is reflected through a series of minor hotel figures and then through the antipathetic but complementary figures of his cousin Gilbert and Sondra; while the part of him that retains some spontaneous feeling is doubled by Roberta, thereby strengthening one's impression that Clyde and Roberta are halves of an uncompleted self, briefly coming together in a poignant unity but lacking the emotional education that would enable them to keep the happiness they have touched. There are more such balancings and modulations, which in their sum endow the novel with a rhythm of necessity.

Reinforcing this narrative rhythm is Dreiser's frequent shifting of his distance from the characters. At some points he establishes an almost intolerable closeness to Clyde, so that we feel locked into the circle of his moods, while at other points he pulls back to convey the sense that Clyde is but another helpless creature among thousands of helpless creatures struggling to get through their time. In the chapters dealing with Clyde upon his arrival at Lycurgus, Dreiser virtually *becomes* his character, narrowing to a hairline the distance between Clyde and himself, in order to make utterly vivid Clyde's pleasure at finding a girl as yielding as Roberta. By contrast, there are sections in which Dreiser looks upon his story from a great height, especially in the chapters after Roberta's death, where his intent is to suggest how impersonal is the working of legal doom and how insignificant Clyde's fate in the larger motions of society. Through these shifts in perspective

Dreiser can show Clyde in his double aspect, both as solitary figure and symbolic agent, confused sufferer and victim of fate.

In the first half of the novel Dreiser prepares us to believe that Clyde *could* commit the crime: which is to say, he prepares us to believe that a part of ourselves could commit the crime. At each point in the boy's development there occurs a meeting between his ill-formed self and the surrounding society. The impoverishment of his family life and the instinctual deprivation of his youth leave him a prey to the values of the streets and the hotels; yet it is a fine stroke on Dreiser's part that only through these tawdry values does Clyde nevertheless become aware of his impoverishment and deprivation. Yearning gives way to cheap desire and false gratification, and these in turn create new and still more incoherent yearnings. It is a vicious circle and the result is not, in any precise sense, a self at all, but rather the beginning of that poisonous fabrication which in America we call a "personality." The hotels are his college, and there he learns to be "insanely eager for all the pleasures which he saw swirling around him." The sterile moralism of his parents cannot provide him with the strength to resist his environment or a principle by which to overcome it. The first tips he receives at the Green-Davidson hotel seem to him "fantastic, Aladdinish really." When he tries to be romantic with his first girl, the images that spring to his mind are of the ornate furnishings in the hotel. Later, as he contemplates killing Roberta, the very idea for the central act in his life comes from casual reading of a newspaper. It would be hard to find in American literature another instance where the passivity, rootlessness, and self-alienation of urban man is so authoritatively presented. For in one sense Clyde does not exist, but is merely a creature of his milieu. And just as in Dreiser's work the problem of human freedom becomes critically acute through a representation of its decline, so the problem of awareness is brought to the forefront through a portrait of its negation.

Even sexuality, which often moves through Dreiser's world like a thick fog, is here diminished and suppressed through the power of social will. Clyde discovers sex as a drugstore clerk, "never weary of observing the beauty, the daring, the self-sufficiency and the sweetness" of the girls who come to his counter. "The wonder of them!" All of these fantasies he then focuses on the commonplace figure of Sondra Finchley, Heloise as a spoiled American girl. Apart from an interval with Roberta, in which he yields to her maternal solicitude, Clyde's sexuality never breaks out as an irresistible force; it is always at the service of his fears, his petty snobbism, his calculations.

Now all of this is strongly imagined, yet what seems still more notable is Dreiser's related intuition that even in a crippled psyche there remain, eager and available, the capacities we associate with a life of awareness. False values stunt and deform these capacities, but in some pitiful way also express and release them. Clyde and Roberta are from the beginning locked in mutual delusion, yet the chapters in which they discover each other are also extremely tender as an unfolding of youthful experience. That this can happen at all suggests how indestructible the life-force is; that Dreiser can portray it in his novels is the reward of his compassion. He is rarely sentimental, he reckons human waste to the bitter end; but at the same time he hovers over these lost and lonely figures, granting them every ounce of true feeling he possibly can, insisting that they too—clerk and shopgirl, quite like intellectual and princess—can know "a kind of ecstasy all out of proportion to the fragile, gim-crack scene" of the Starlight Amusement Park.

Dreiser surrenders himself to the emotional life of his figures, not by passing over their delusions or failures but by casting all his energy into evoking the fullness of their experience. And how large, finally, is the sense of the human that smolders in this book! How unwavering the feeling for "the sensitive and seeking individual in his pitiful struggle with nature—with his enormous urges and his pathetic equipment!" Dreiser's passion for detail is a passion for his subject; his passion for his subject, a passion for the suffering of men. As we are touched by Clyde's early affection for Roberta, so later we participate vicariously in his desperation to be rid of her. We share this desire with some shame, but unless we count ourselves among the hopelessly pure, we share it.

Other naturalists, when they show a character being destroyed by overwhelming forces, frequently leave us with a sense of littleness and helplessness, as if the world were collapsed. Of Dreiser that is not, in my own experience, true. For he is always on the watch for a glimmer of transcendence, always concerned with the possibility of magnitude. Clyde is pitiable, his life and fate are pitiable; yet at the end we feel a somber exaltation, for we know that *An American Tragedy* does not seek to persuade us that human existence need be without value or beauty.

No, for Dreiser life is something very different. What makes him so absorbing a novelist, despite grave faults, is that he remains endlessly open to experience. This is something one cannot say easily about most modern writers, including those more subtle and gifted than Dreiser. The trend of modern literature has often been toward a recoil from experience, a nausea before its flow, a denial of its worth. Dreiser, to be sure, is unable to make the finer discriminations among varieties of experience; and there is no reason to expect these from him. But he is marvelous in his devotion to whatever portion of life a man can have; marvelous in his conviction that something sacred resides even in the transience of our days; marvelous in his feeling that the grimmest of lives retain the possibility of "a mystic something of beauty that perennially transfigures the world." Transfigures—that is the key word, and not the catch-phrases of mechanistic determinism he furnished his detractors.

Santayana, in his lecture on Spinoza, speaks of "one of the most important and radical of religious perceptions":

> It has perceived that though it is living, it is powerless to live; that though it may die, it is powerless to die; and that altogether, at every instant and in every particular, it is in the hands of some alien and inscrutable power.
>
> Of this felt power I profess to know nothing further. To me, as yet, it is merely the counterpart of my impotence. I should not venture, for instance, to call this power almighty, since I have no means of knowing how much it can do: but I should not hesitate, if I may coin a word, to call it *omnificent*: it is to me, by definition, the doer of everything that is done. I am not asserting the physical validity of this sense of agency or cause: I am merely feeling the force, the friendliness, the hostility, the unfathomableness of the world.

Dreiser, I think, would have accepted these words, for the power of which Santayana speaks is the power that flows, in all its feverish vibration, through *An American Tragedy*.

Julian Markels

Dreiser and the Plotting of Inarticulate Experience

If one thinks that such thoughts do not come to so common a type of mind—that such feelings require a higher mental development— I would urge for their consideration the fact that it is the higher mental development that does away with such thoughts. It is the higher mental development which induces philosophy and that fortitude which refuses to dwell upon such things—refuses to be made to suffer by their consideration. The common type of mind is exceedingly keen on all matters which relate to its physical welfare—exceedingly keen. It is the unintellectual miser who sweats blood at the loss of a hundred dollars. It is the Epictetus who smiles when the last vestige of physical welfare is removed.

Sister Carrie

By now the cataloguing of Dreiser's limitations has settled into a rather dry routine: his turgid and graceless style, which led F. R. Leavis to observe that Dreiser writes as if he hasn't a native language; his limited insight into the psychology of his characters; his wearisome attention to detail; and his editorial pretentiousness and inconsistency, in which he often seems bent on making metaphysical mountains out of mechanistic molehills. Such characteristics are not mere superfluous gimcrackery but part of Dreiser's substance, inseparable from his fictional method and from the conception of human experience that he attempts to shape in his fiction. Yet to pigeonhole Dreiser in this way is to obscure the fact that not all of his substance is composed of such defects. Equally the product of his method and conception, when he is at his best, is a powerful sense of the mystery underlying human experience, of the fathomless processes which hold our lives in suspension, of the deep sources of pain and desire with which our human condition confronts us—in short, of what Dreiser himself called the wonder of life. Even if he is not a Balzac or a Dickens or a Dostoevsky, the whole of Dreiser's substance is frequently rich

Reprinted from *The Massachusetts Review,* II, #3 (Spring 1961), 431-34, 440-48, by permission. Copyright © 1961 The Massachusetts Review, Inc.

and moving and powerful. It is time finally to acknowledge him as our own and go on from there—to explore his quality and unravel his meaning for us. If we cannot afford to ignore his limitations, neither can we afford to let him lie bound in that literary dungeon to which he has been consigned for some years by the neoliberal Zeuses of contemporary criticism.

The greatest obstacle in the way of such an enterprise is not that Dreiser writes as if he hasn't a native language, but that as critics we are unprepared to pass beyond that fact. We are disconcerted to read a statement like Saul Bellow's in his review of F. O. Matthiessen's book on Dreiser: "But it is very odd that no one has thought to ask just what the 'bad writing' of a powerful novelist signifies." Such a remark suggests that in some significant way we are estranged from the novel as a literary form, that to recover Dreiser we must recover the suppleness of certain critical faculties which have been until recently the victims of atrophy.

The first, if indirect step, in such a recovery is to confront the fact that Dreiser's artistic purposes made no strenuous demands upon his style, which after all may be true of a novelist though not of a poet. Dreiser could on occasion produce a kind of "good writing," so that his characteristic style is the result not only of ineptness but of a choice of relevant means for communicating what he had to. At scattered moments in his writing there is a compactness and fluency which usually passes unnoticed. There is, for example, this paragraph from *An American Tragedy:*

> The impact of this remark, a reflection of the exact truth, was not necessary to cause Clyde to gaze attentively, and even eagerly. For apart from her local position and means and taste in dress and manners, Sondra was of the exact order and spirit that most intrigued him—a somewhat refined (and because of means and position showered upon her) less savage, although scarcely less self-centered, Hortense Briggs. She was, in her small, intense way, a seeking Aphrodite, eager to prove to any who were sufficiently attractive the destroying power of her charm, while at the same time retaining her own personality and individuality free of any entangling alliance or compromise. However, for varying reasons which she could not quite explain to herself, Clyde appealed to her. He might not be anything socially or financially, but he was interesting to her.

Eliminate the flatulent next-to-last sentence, change the parenthetical into a subordinate clause, and you have in this passage a piece of smooth and deliberate prose such as might have been written by an imitator of Henry James. Just as it stands the passage has a liveliness and precision which, if more prevalent, would make Dreiser's style less vulnerable to attack. But such writing is not frequent and hence not memorable in Dreiser; and indeed, he writes in this way only when, as in the present instance, he is taking time out to summarize previously recounted information. When his eye is on his main business his ear goes flat, and he characteristically writes the thick prose by which we remember him.

The source of his power and his meaning for us lies elsewhere, then, and I think it is in his method of arranging the episodes of his plots in order to dramatize with perfect coherence that absence of foreordained purpose in the universe, and its corollary, the hegemony of chance, of which he speaks so awkwardly in his "philosophical" writings. Not consistently but in long and powerful sequences, Dreiser's plot construction results in a fully credible image of human experience as an amoral process; it implies the possibility of human purpose and dignity arising out of a necessary immersion in this process; and hence Dreiser's method excludes the deterministic pathos of the conventional naturalistic novel, which conceives of human experience as the closing of a trap rather than the unfolding of a process. Frequently in Dreiser's novels the moment-to-moment action gives us no reason to desire or expect either good or bad fortune for the characters, no reason to feel hopeful, fearful, sad, or angry on their behalf. We are convinced instead that for them whatever is, is right; and we are moved by the mystery of their experience being so coherently purposeless and yet possibly resulting for them in an enlargement of being. When we see Carrie Meeber respond to her experience directly in fear and desire, without imposing upon it any moral categories or expectations, when we see her enlarge her worldly status and her human identity by her unquestioning submission to the "whatever is" of her experience, then we know why Dreiser attributes to Carrie the quality of "emotional greatness." When we see Hurstwood and Clyde Griffiths ruined by an equally emotional and unquestioning submission, then perhaps we know in a glimmer what Dreiser must have meant by the mystery and terror and wonder of life.

Such knowledge arises from a rhythm in the sequence of Dreiser's episodes rather than from anything that can be communicated by a graceful style. It is the rhythm of inarticulate human experience, undifferentiated and hence by definition without style. Matthiessen suggested rightly that Dreiser's sea imagery, his symbol of the rocking chair, and his own fondness for a rocking chair, all point to "a physical basis for the rhythm of his thoughts." But where the imagery and symbols are only its symptoms, the "physical basis" itself is established by Dreiser's method of construction, which is his true source of strength. It is also the source of his weakness, as I will indicate later, in that his method of construction disables Dreiser from portraying the emergence in human experience of moral consciousness and its corollary, literary style.

*   *   *

In 1916 Dreiser described to H. L. Mencken how he began writing *Sister Carrie:*

> Finally—September 1899 I took a piece of yellow paper and to please him [Arthur Henry] wrote down a title at random—*Sister Carrie*—and began. From September to Oct. 15th or thereabouts I wrote steadily to where Carrie met Hurstwood. Then I quit, disgusted. I thought it was rotten.

Whether or not his critics agree with Dreiser, this section of the novel has never commanded their attention. Their general impression seems to be that he outgrew the fumbling methods of composition that characterize his earliest work. It is all the more striking, then, to notice that Dreiser employs precisely the method I have described in what are perhaps the two most admired sequences in all his novels, the decline of Hurstwood in *Sister Carrie*, and, twenty-five years and five novels later, the events in *An American Tragedy* beginning with Clyde Griffiths' arrival in upstate New York and ending with the drowning of Roberta Alden.

The long grade of Hurstwood's decline is so familiar that I will not rehearse its details here. The little episode where he decides to turn on the gas but hasn't money for a flophouse room in which to do it, then begs a quarter, then decides to use the money for food and carry on awhile longer, is typical of the whole sequence and identical in design to the earlier episodes involving Carrie. The sequence in *An American Tragedy* warrants attention, however, because it shows the fundamental character of Dreiser's plastic power unchanged after the major span of his writing career, and because it may serve to clear up a traditional misunderstanding of the form and underlying conception of that novel. Everybody knows that Dreiser was using a murder case reported in the papers, the drowning of Grace Brown by Chester Gillette in Moose Lake, New York, in 1906. When Dreiser locates the drowning two-thirds through the 800-page novel, having told in minute detail the grim story of his hero's life beginning at age twelve, critics on the scent of naturalism assume that he has been spending his time building up a great weight of environmental forces that are to crush Clyde and explain the murder. But none of the mountainous information about Clyde's early life is even relevant to explain the murder. His early history interests us in the same way the first chapters of a biography do, as a segment in the total process of a man's life. The murder is fully explained by the events immediately leading up to it, beginning with Clyde's arrival in Lycurgus. It is the perfectly logical result of a process which is again exhibited in Dreiser's method of arranging his episodes. Only this time, as befits the amoral character of that process, the hero emerges at the ebb rather than the flow of fortune.

After a boyhood with "the flavor of sand," to use Alfred Kazin's phrase for Dreiser's own boyhood, Clyde Griffiths is brought to Lycurgus, New York, to work in the shrinking room of his uncle's collar factory. At first he forms social attachments with people of his own class; but once he has glimpsed the elegant and genteel world of his cousins and Sondra Finchley, he snobbishly fancies himself above his former friends and cuts himself off from them. But then his cousins and Sondra go off for their summer holidays, leaving Clyde isolated and lonely at the time when Roberta Alden arrives on the scene. Clyde and Roberta form an attachment, and as their romance develops he persuades her to move and take a room with a private entrance. Roberta no sooner compromises herself by this action than Sondra returns to town and arranges to have Clyde invited out in high society. Then, at the moment when Clyde has finally "arrived" socially, Roberta, who now looks faded compared to Sondra but whom Clyde has been seeing and deceiving out of pity and guilt, discovers that she is pregnant.

All the remaining details—the series of attempts to get an abortion, Clyde's refusal to marry Roberta, his planning of the murder—are arranged in the same pattern. Like Carrie, Clyde is shuttled ceaselessly back and forth. Unequipped to anticipate or judge his experience by previously formulated standards, he responds logically to each circumstance as it arises, taking his

facts one by one. At no single point before the end of the sequence
are we well enough informed to pass judgment on what is happening. But at the end no judgment is possible. Everybody—Clyde,
Samuel Griffiths, Sondra, Roberta—has been moderately but not
unduly selfish. Like Drouet, each one has merely performed according to his *gestalt*. If anybody had taken a firm stand at any single
point, catastrophe might have been averted. But nothing in the
situation facing any single character has indicated the necessity
for such a stand. By his characteristic arrangement of episodes,
Dreiser creates a firm pattern for the inscrutable, patternless drift
of experience.

I do not mean to deny, however, that Clyde Griffiths and
Hurstwood before him are "victims." Indeed, it is perhaps more
forlorn and helpless to be a victim of the blind drift of cosmic
chance than of the determinate and hence remediable forces en-
gendered by society. But it is also more dignified, and truer to the
condition of being human rather than a laboratory animal. In
Dreiser's sense we are all victims equally, so that the fact when
applied to Hurstwood or Clyde Griffiths is merely a *donnée* of
their existence, not a special occasion for pity or anger on their
behalf. In the article on "The Curious Shifts of the Poor" from
which much of the account of Hurstwood's decline is taken,
Dreiser ends his description of the Bowery *Lumpenproletariat* by
saying, "the individuals composing this driftwood are no more
miserable than others." They and Hurstwood are no more victims
than Carrie, who drifts upward instead of downward. And when
Dreiser claims for Carrie the quality of "emotional greatness," he
implies that it is not mere chance that her victimization should
lead to success and Hurstwood's to death. He implies that a purposive and meaningful life may emerge from the meaningless drift
of experience, and with it a personal "style" which might in turn
demand embodiment by an appropriate literary style. And it is
precisely at the point where he tries to fill out this implication,
to dramatize the emergence of consciousness, purpose and style,
that we may discover the limitations of Dreiser's method and his
genuine weakness as a novelist.

To fully perceive this weakness, first we must make what I
believe is a Dreiserian distinction between being articulate and
being conscious. A person may be articulate in learning to recognize his desires, to name them, and to pursue their objects actively
instead of passively. Consciousness requires further the ability to

judge those desires, to anticipate the consequences of pursuing them for some larger system of values, and hence to become responsible for one's active choices. To grow from articulateness into consciousness is to step from an amoral into a moral world of experience; and it is precisely in portraying that step that Dreiser's method proves inadequate. The method works successfully only when the characters are, so to speak, below the threshold of consciousness. It works successfully to bring Clyde Griffiths to the murder at the end of Book Two of *An American Tragedy*. Then Book Three is devoted mainly to Clyde's debate with himself (and Dreiser's debate with us) whether he should become conscious of the implications of his act and accept responsibility for it. In *Sister Carrie* the method works successfully to the point where Carrie prefers Hurstwood to Drouet. And it is most significant that once Dreiser brings Carrie to that point, he does not know what to do with her, and shifts the entire focus of the novel from her rise to Hurstwood's decline, where again the method works successfully to record a fall below the threshold of consciousness into an undifferentiated state of being comparable to Carrie's at the beginning. Carrie's rise during the second half of the novel is so clearly directed toward the emergence of consciousness that we have no reason to doubt Dreiser's intention here. This crucial result of her immersion in the drift of experience is pointed at and argued. But it never acquires sufficient dramatic weight to balance Hurstwood's decline. The ultimate weakness of *Sister Carrie* is the thinness and lack of warmth, the pasteboard quality of the heroine during the last half of the novel. For Dreiser was unwilling, perhaps unable, to find a method for depicting the manifestations of Carrie's enhanced powers in conscious and morally responsible actions.

Dreiser's tenacity in clinging to his characteristic method forces him to give increasingly inconsistent accounts of Carrie once she begins reaping the fruits of her career. The ripest fruit in her harvest is her relationship with Ames, who is introduced at Carrie's final stage of development as an unmistakable representative of the conscious life. She has only a few brief conversations with this shadowy young man, who "seemed wiser than Hurstwood, saner and brighter than Drouet," in his belief that self-aggrandizement is mere vanity, that one must read important books rather than sentimental novels, and that finally one must be selfless. In their last talk, after Carrie has become a successful comedienne, Ames urges her to give up comedy and try for serious parts, where her talents will be more valuable to others and will therefore endure:

> . . . You have this quality in your eyes and mouth and in your nature. You can lose it, you know. If you turn away from it and live to satisfy yourself alone, it will go fast enough. The look will leave your eyes. Your mouth will change. Your power to act will disappear. You may think they won't, but they will. Nature takes care of that.

Here is Carrie's final attainment, the knowledge that if she lives only to satisfy herself she will lose herself. Her ceaseless drifting toward only what satisfies herself has led her to confront finally the demand of Nature that she consciously shape her experience to run in the channels of selflessness. Here more than anywhere in Dreiser is the justification for Eliseo Vivas' remark that "there is more to his own concrete dramatic picture of men and society than he finds room for in his mechanistic philosophy." But it is also true that at this moment Dreiser's dramatic picture is not very roomy either. In the sketchy characterization of Ames we have another instance of Dreiser's intention made perfectly clear but not rendered dramatically effective. And in his refusal to let Carrie take up the challenge of Ames' suggestion, he is squelching her arbitrarily. We have watched her ascend from the Hansons to Drouet and from Drouet to Hurstwood. Now, when Hurstwood is left behind and Ames appears, Dreiser becomes fussy and hesitant at the prospect of making Carrie as conscious and responsible as Ames challenges her to be.

Indeed, as if the record of Carrie's relation with Ames were not already sufficiently thin and halting, in other passages late in the novel Dreiser undermines Ames' position and the resolution which Ames proposes to Carrie. Dreiser allows Carrie brief glimmerings of consciousness, but only to remember her early career in Chicago in terms that attribute to it a rationale as thoroughly inconsistent with the facts as Ames's challenge and the entire role he plays are consistent. When Hurstwood stops looking for a job, Carrie remembers scornfully that in her early struggle in Chicago she never stopped trying; she decides that now, as in Chicago, she will try to get an acting job "as a last resort in distress." The facts are that although she did struggle valiantly in Chicago, she also eventually stopped trying, and was ready to pack up and go home when Drouet rescued her; and that her Chicago venture as an amateur actress was not a last resort in distress (though she had begun to tire of Drouet), but something arranged entirely by Drouet, signed, sealed and delivered on a platter without Carrie's lifting a finger. Dreiser makes her remember these things as if she had planned and pursued her goals systematically. And this engrafted rationale leads him into a damaging confusion in his final portrait of Carrie. Near the end of the novel, long after her last interview with Ames, and after her resounding success on the comic stage has brought her a salary of $150 a week, we are told:

> It does not take money long to make plain its impotence, providing the desires are in the realm of affection. With her one hundred and fifty in hand, Carrie could think of nothing particular to do. . . . Her clothes had for some time been wholly satisfactory. Another day or two and she would receive another hundred and fifty. It began to appear as if this were not so startlingly necessary to maintain her present state. If she wanted to do anything better or move higher, she must have more—a great deal more.

For most of her life her desires were in fact in the realm of money. But now that her experience with Ames has transformed them into desires for affection, now that money has shown its impotence, she decides she must have more money.[1] The whole paragraph until the last sentence is a confirmation in her own experience of what Ames had told her. But instead of letting her mind drift in characteristic fashion to memories of Ames, as earlier it drifted to Drouet or Hurstwood in similar situations, now Dreiser intervenes with a false explanation which makes Carrie inaccessible to the wisdom derived from her own immersion in the drift of experience. Dreiser increasingly stiffens to resist the deepest implications of his own method as that method threatens to project Carrie across the threshold of consciousness into the arms, so to speak, of Ames.

Thus at the beginning of his career in *Sister Carrie* and at its height in *An American Tragedy*, Dreiser balks at portraying the

---

[1] There are objections to my reading here, on the grounds that "more" is ambiguous or even that it refers clearly to "affection" rather than "money." I can only rely on an ear which I hope is by now attuned to Dreiser's syntactical ambiguities, on other evidence for exactly the same kind of confusion in the later characterization of Carrie, and on the whole of the last sentence quoted. In that sentence, "better," "higher," and "more" all refer to "her present state." And Carrie's "present state" is founded on clothes and money, not affection.

life of consciousness and responsibility which arises logically out of his own conception of the inarticulate drift of experience. He arbitrarily qualifies Carrie's emergence into consciousness, and later he can do no more than make Clyde Griffiths' similar emergence the subject of an essentially unresolved debate. And without a dramatically rendered life of moral consciousnes there is no demand for style. There is in fact an implicit denial of style, so that finally it is accurate to say that Dreiser's style is the necessary defect of his virtue. In its meandering syntax, its fuzzy diction, its jerky rhythms and abrupt transitions, Dreiser's style is almost wholly unarticulated. And in this respect it simply affirms the inarticulateness of his characters. A coherently inflected style would attribute to the characters a personal "style" appropriate only to a degree of consciousness that Dreiser does not allow them; it would arrest the flow of experience created by his method of plotting; it would embody the results of the process rather than the process under way. Dreiser's own style actually helps to articulate his vision of life as an amoral process containing its own coherent rhythm, bearing us along mysteriously and challenging us to become conscious of ourselves.

The somehow unexpected power achieved despite his style by Dreiser's method of plotting may serve to remind us of the enormous resources of the novel as a genre. We often hear nowadays that the novel is dead or dying, having exhausted its materials, with the possible exception of those relating to the condition of the self. Dreiser's power is unexpected because he is not directly concerned with the self, because in his gallery of characters there is so little of that "self-presence" which Ortega y Gasset told us is the sign of greatness in the novel and the one necessity for its continuance as a literary genre. Dreiser's novels do not bear the sign of greatness, but they show how various and new may be the novel's sources of life, for they derive their vitality precisely from Dreiser's ability to portray human experience before "self-presence" is achieved, to portray human beings in the process of becoming differentiated and conscious of themselves.

Dreiser's portrayal may remind us too that we still struggle to become conscious of ourselves and to locate the responsibilities that genuinely arise from our condition of life. It is traditional to compare Dreiser to James and find him parochial and thick-headed in his inability to portray the conscious life. But the social facts out of which James was able to imagine the conscious and moral life simply did not exist for Dreiser. And they do not exist for us. Dreiser's facts, which are our facts, are still largely inscrutable. And Dreiser's parochialism is simply part of a national phenomenon in our life and letters during this century, from the aloof clinical observation of the unconscious life in Stephen Crane's *Maggie* to the forced rejection of the conscious life in the novels of Ernest Hemingway. We smile nowadays to think how Dreiser's great contemporary Clarence Darrow made a monkey out of Bryan at the Scopes Trial. We too often forget the enormous waste of Darrow's granite courage and high intelligence engaged at the level of such monkeyshines. It is Dreiser's distinction that, despite his personal philosophy, as an artist he was often able to cut beneath the parochial oversimplifications of his time—from Social Darwinism and Zolaism to *nada* and Marxism and the honor of the South—to a core of substance that remains a central preoccupation of our best contemporary novelists. One might almost say that writers like Saul Bellow and Herbert Gold pick up where Dreiser left off, trying to discover by their art the point at which emerges from the amoral drift of experience a universal content for our proper consciousness of ourselves, the conditions under which we might honestly assume our responsibilities. Where Dreiser was able to imagine coherently the processes of experience but not the self-presence of his characters, the younger writers create characters superbly endowed with self-presence but still searching to attune themselves to the fundamental processes of human experience. Such writers may be said to represent the conscience of America. And that is why, for this reader, to look back at the American novel in the twentieth century is to find Dreiser, with his stubborn yet hopeful challenge to immerse ourselves in the dark processes of life, standing at the center of the field of vision.

Of Crime and Punishment

For American fiction, the nineteen-twenties inaugurated a more flourishing period than any Dreiser had previously known. Several of his near contemporaries were coming into their own with a wider public. His most devoted followers, especially Sherwood Anderson, were growing up around him. Among the many new talents which made this decade one of the richest in our literary history, both realists like Sinclair Lewis and naturalists like Dos Passos were conscious of how much Dreiser had helped to prepare their way. It is more surprising to find Scott Fitzgerald saying, at the dawn of his own career: "I consider H. L. Mencken and Theodore Dreiser the greatest men living in the country today."

Dreiser took a varying and complex attitude towards the dominant mood of the 'twenties. He joined in their sweeping arraignment of the past and present inadequacies of American culture, and said flatly: "We are not an artistic nation. All we care about is to be rich and powerful." But this conviction did not lead him, as it did so many younger artists, to flight and exile. The roots of his own life were now inextricably intertwined with half a century of American experience, and, though he noted that much he had gone through had been "inimical to mental freedom and artistic energy," he still could declare America to be "as satisfying to me, as stimulating, I am sure, as Russia ever was to Tolstoy or Dostoevsky . . . or France to Flaubert or de Maupassant."

These examples indicate his realization—out of a wider range of reference than he had previously possessed—that the artist's adjustment to society is never likely to be easy. He was sympathetic with social protest, but reaffirmed his belief that the greatest writers "are not concerned with social amelioration as an end or a motive. Rather their purpose is to present life in the round, good, bad, and indifferent, alike, without thought of change and without hope of improvement. They paint the thing as it is, leaving change to nature or to others." In an introduction to a new edition of *Tono-Bungay* he strongly preferred Wells the novelist to Wells the reformer. This preference was naturally colored by Dreiser's own recurrent doubts of all efforts to order the world. "As I see him," he stated again in this introduction, "man is much more led or pushed than he is leading or pushing."

He admired the new fiction for the frankness of its record, yet in another twist of mood he saw a serious limitation in its lack of "exaltation." He was also puzzled by the fact that so many of this next generation of realists wanted "to indict life, not picture it in its ordinary beauty. . . . What is lacking in the experience of these young writers to make them think there is no beauty?" By observing where Dreiser believed "beauty" and "exaltation" were now to be found, we may begin to catch the tone of the long novel upon which he was at work and which he hoped would provide what the decade was missing. Beauty did not exist for him in delicate or fragile isolation. He described his characteristic associations with it when he voiced his appreciation of the essays of Llewellyn Powys: "They are so serious, so pathetic, so—in the main—sombre and so beautiful. They are so full of a genuine understanding of life and of a kind of sane sorrow because of the fact that in general things are so necessitous, so hopeless, and so unrewarded. And yet there is a courageous and hence impressive joy in the amazing and ebullient beauty that informs the necessitous and inexplicable and unescapable process which we know as living."

Beauty was to be seized at the heart of tragedy, as was also exaltation: "If there are all the chain cigar stores, chain drug stores, haberdasheries, movie theatres, and big hotels in Manhattan to describe, here are also Hell, Heaven, and Purgatory of the soul." But contemporary writers, held too close by the details of surface description, "rarely climb any such heights as Dante climbed to look out over the tremendous waste of lives." Dreiser had none of the firmness of vision to emulate even from afar *The Divine Comedy*. But he must have been conscious of the fact that he was summoning up all his resources when he changed the title of his novel from *Mirage* to *An American Tragedy*. In an interview in 1921, in which he looked back to his situation at the time of *Sister Carrie*, he revealed the point of view that was to be dominant in his treatment of Clyde Griffiths: "I never can and never want to bring myself to the place where I can ignore the sensitive and seeking individual in his pitiful struggle with nature—with his enormous urges and his pathetic equipment."

Dreiser worked longer and more steadily upon this novel than upon any of his others. This concentration was made possible by the fact that Liveright—who had now brought all his works together under one imprint and in 1923 had reissued *The "Genius"*—was providing him with a four-thousand-dollar annual drawing account. He wrote, as always, with great uncertainty and difficulty. But he had chosen his subject deliberately, and was sure that it was not only right for what he wanted to say, but also very typical of American life. When he had revisited Terre Haute in 1915, he had stayed at the same hotel to which his mother had once come looking for work. He recalled how his brother Rome used sometimes to put on the best clothes he had and idle outside the doorway with a toothpick in his mouth to give the impression that he had just dined there. Looking around the midnight grill, Dreiser watched those the community would call "our most successful men," men "of a solid, resonant, generative materiality. The flare of the cloth of their suits! The blaze of their skins and eyes! The hardy, animal implication of their eyes!" These were lesser Cowperwoods, and Dreiser continued to be attracted by them.

"But," he went on, "what interested me more, and this was sad too, were the tribes and shoals of the incomplete, the botched, the semi-articulate, all hungry and helpless, who never get to come to a place like this at all—who yearn for a taste of this show and flare and never attain to the least taste of it." These were the opposites of Cowperwood, of Dreiser's American version of the surviving fittest. From these other ranks he was to pick Clyde Griffiths, but he would give him a taste of the wealth from which he was excluded, and the weak boy, more sensitive than most and thus more helpless, would be destroyed by it.

In one sense, Dreiser was taking one of the stock legends of American behavior and reversing its happy ending. After the novel's appearance in 1925 he said: "The type of life that produced it has not changed. For years I have been arrested in stories and plays by the poor young man who marries the rich man's daughter. I have had many letters from people who wrote: 'Clyde Griffiths might have been me.'"

He was also writing a documentary novel, as he did in his study of the businessman. But here the core of his material was even more public—not the story of financial operations that a

Yerkes would keep as hidden as he could, but what everybody was reading in the newspapers, indeed, the favorite drama of the American people: the story of a murder trial. After pondering several other cases he chose for his document the drowning of Grace Brown by Chester Gillette in Moose Lake, Herkimer County, New York, in 1906. Dreiser's center of interest, to be sure, was not in crime and its detection, but in contemplating a victim of the contemporary American dream. Clyde Griffiths' aspirations to rise in the world, to be a success as measured by money and social position, were those stimulated and sanctioned by twentieth-century capitalist society, and Dreiser instinctively moved his climax, without specifying any dates, into the showy period after the First World War. Before the glittering possibility of marrying Sondra Finchley had flashed upon him, Clyde had become involved, out of his loneliness and repression, in an affair with the mill girl Roberta Alden. If he had had some money of his own, he might have handled the unlooked-for consequence —Roberta's pregnancy—as the harder and more experienced young men of the social set knew how to. But Clyde was caught, and thrashed about in a hopeless effort to escape. What Dreiser studied was the sexual and social forces that overpowered Clyde and swept him before them until, seeing no way out, in his shallow immaturity he finally plotted murder. Yet Roberta's actual death was accidental, since the boat into which Clyde lured her upon the lake overturned at a moment when he had not willed it. The ultimate range of Dreiser's theme thereby became the terrible and baffling problem of justice.

His chief addition to his sources was his detailed presentation, in the first of the three books of his novel, of Clyde's background. The Gillette family, though not wealthy, were not really poor. But Dreiser, in order to carry Clyde's actions beyond the sphere of any merely temperamental aberration, immersed the Griffiths family in poverty as extreme as his own youth had known. As a result, Clyde's world, from the time we first see him as a boy of twelve until his death, is portrayed with a more deliberate and more detailed thoroughness than that of any of Dreiser's other characters. Dreiser shows him as always worked upon by his environment and circumstances, even to the point of being tempted to murder by coming across a newspaper account of a drowning.

In the opening scene he is an unwilling participant in the street service conducted by his preacher father in connection with the itinerant Bible mission he runs. For this vague imprac-

tical father Dreiser drew in part upon Asa Conklin, his employer
in his first job after his year at college, who had been equally
vague and impractical in his schemes for promoting real estate.
The emotional center of the Griffiths family is Clyde's mother,
who buoys up her husband by her wholehearted if ignorant faith.
But Clyde is from the start alien to their values. He observes
that his parents are forever proclaiming the care of God for all,
and yet they are always "hard up": "Plainly there was something wrong somewhere." Beginning in this fashion Dreiser
makes a sustained contrast between the professed and the actual,
as it strikes a boy who will have little regular education and no
accurate training for anything.

Each successive episode is designed by Dreiser for its bearing
upon Clyde's final tragedy. For instance, his older sister Esta, as
tired of the dreariness of their life as he is ("dreary" is one of
the recurrent key words here), runs away with a lover. In spite
of his parents' grief, Clyde, now in his adolescence, cannot see
that "her going was such a calamity, not from the *going* point
of view at any rate." Then she is deserted and comes back, and
Clyde reflects that this is typical of everything that happens
in the family, of their repeated rhythm of failure. But as she
bears her illegitimate child, Clyde cannot share in the stock emo-
tion of blaming the whole affair upon the seducer. His confused
mixture of feelings foreshadows what they will be in his own
affair with Roberta.

The section of this first book that has been praised most often
is where Dreiser evokes the splendor for which Clyde longs by
making him a bell-hop in the Green-Davidson in Kansas City.
The vast luxury hotel is a peculiarly fitting symbol for the
glamour and the waste of the modern American city, as Henry
James had observed in *The American Scene*. Dreiser's way of
conveying its spell over Clyde is one of the most matured examples of his method. He is more detached than when he wrote
Sister Carrie. He can now judge as "gauche" all the senseless
overfurnishing which is "without the saving grace of either
simplicity or necessity." But his richly stored memory can create
to the full Clyde's own amazement and awe at "this perfectly
marvellous-marvellous realm." Dreiser is so sympathetically involved with how everything here would strike Clyde's starved
imagination that he can take us through the routine of a bellhop's day as though, once again, it were something out of *The
Arabian Nights*. The downpour of small change into his hand

"seemed fantastic, Aladdinish really." Dreiser can make us feel what Clyde feels, even through the trite image Clyde uses when complimenting his first girl friend Hortense: " 'An' your eyes are just like soft, black velvet," he persisted eagerly. 'They're wonderful.' He was thinking of an alcove in the Green-Davidson hung with black velvet."

But the main reason why Dreiser can make us feel touched by Clyde's feelings is that he is aware of how pathetic they really are. For Clyde this hotel is the actual world in contrast with his family's shakily based ideal. But Dreiser, with a firmness of balance he had never quite possessed before, can let us sense at the same time how hopelessly wrong Clyde is in believing that these surroundings mark "a social superiority almost unbelievable." Dreiser observes that here was the "most dangerous" environment for the boy's temperament that could have been found. He was so "insanely eager for all the pleasures which he imagined he saw swirling around him." His "none-too-discerning" mind could so easily be convinced that the chief end of life was having and spending money.

This first book ends with Clyde's initial disaster. A car in which he is riding with a group of the other bell-hops and their girls runs down a child; and Clyde, knowing that the scandal will cost him his job, decides to skip out of town. We see him next three years later, twenty now and very cautious, working at the Union League Club in Chicago. Here by chance he encounters the uncle whom he had envisaged distantly as a "kind of Croesus," Samuel Griffiths, a collar manufacturer of Lycurgus, New York. He is favorably impressed by Clyde's quiet good looks, and, feeling also some compunction over his previous neglect of his brother's family, he listens to the young man's request that he be given an opportunity to make his way in the mill. The shift to an upstate New York town of twenty-five thousand affords Dreiser another sphere in which to demonstrate how completely he has worked out the details of the world in which he has placed Clyde.

He has studied once again the gradations of the economic and social scale. Though secretly somewhat awed by the bigger men he meets in Chicago, in Lycurgus Samuel Griffiths is at the top. The self-made founder of his own business, he already represents a degree of solid conservatism not yet attained by the families of even newer enterprises, such as the Finchley Electric Sweepers. Dreiser also makes a telling contrast between Mr. Griffiths, who is in general tolerant and forbearing, and his son Gilbert, who is self-centered, vain, and meanly arrogant. This is the same kind of difference Dreiser noted in *Jennie Gerhardt* between Archibald and Robert Kane. Eisenstein, whose script for a picture based on *An American Tragedy* was not what Paramount wanted, seized upon the significance of the contrast. He saw that in Mr. Griffiths "there still prevails the patriarchal democratic spirit of the fathers, who have not forgotten how they themselves came to the town in rags to make their fortunes. The succeeding generation is already approximating to a money aristocracy; and in this connection it is interesting to note the difference in attitude towards Clyde adopted by his uncle and his cousin respectively." Mr. Griffiths takes it for granted that Clyde should have his chance; Gilbert regards him as an interloper who should be kept out of their inner circle.

Another telling contrast, which occupies Clyde's thoughts through most of the long second book, is between Roberta and Sondra. Roberta is like Clyde in that her whole youth has been grounded in poverty. She has come from her father's farm to work in the mill, afflicted by the same "virus of ambition and unrest" that afflicts Clyde. Until she meets him she still feels herself terribly alone. And when he, as the foreman of the shop in which she is working, begins to show an interest in her, she looks up to him as someone far outside her sphere. This is one of Dreiser's most effective strokes in pointing out the successive rungs of insecurity. For Clyde at this moment is aware that he has not really been accepted by Sondra's family and that he stands firmly nowhere.

The developing relationship between them, entered upon with misgivings by both, is handled with Dreiser's greatest tenderness. He knows how, in their first happiness together, they will feel at the Starlight Amusement Park "a kind of ecstasy all out of proportion to the fragile, gimcrack scene." He is equally in possession of Roberta's whole state of mind from her first deep sense of guilt at yielding herself to Clyde to her agonized realization that she can no longer hold him. The crisis when she discovers that she is going to have a baby, and when Clyde tries in vain to find a doctor who will perform an abortion, is regarded by Dreiser as "an illustration of the enormous handicaps imposed by ignorance, youth, poverty and fear." Dreiser knows Roberta thoroughly, and Clyde's vision of her "steady, accusing, horrified, innocent blue eyes" is likely to remain with the reader as long as anything in the novel.

The contrast with Sondra Finchley is revelatory in more ways than Dreiser seems to have meant it to be. From the first moment Clyde sees her with his cousins, she appears to him "as smart and vain and sweet a girl" as he has ever laid eyes on. These curiously mixed adjectives suggest the quality of the social group in which she is at the center, a faster-moving and more stylish group than is quite approved by the rather conservative Griffiths. Clyde reads about her avidly in the society columns until she decides one day to take him up "as a lark," partly because she realizes how much this will irritate his cousin Gilbert. At this point Clyde determines to break off with Roberta, only to discover that it is already too late. Sondra soon realizes that she is really attracted by Clyde. She is flattered at first by his doglike devotion, but gradually responds to an intensity in him beyond that of the college boys she is used to. But what Clyde finds in his "baby-talking girl" is what Dreiser never manages to convey to us concretely.

Here is the clearest-cut instance of what we have noted recurrently in Dreiser's portrayal of women. He was able to give reality to the kind he had known when he was young. But as soon as he reached above a certain point in the social scale, the details seem superficial and the total effect false. By the mid-nineteen-twenties he had doubtless known many flappers like Sondra, but he still could not make them actual. We therefore have here a strangely double effect. We know what Sondra symbolizes for Clyde, but it is as though we were looking at her from a distance, through the language of the society columns or the eyes of the outsider who does not really understand her. In part this may have been what Dreiser intended. When Clyde attempts to explain at the end the overwhelming fascination Sondra exercised over him, he says: "She seemed to know more than anyone else I ever knew." We have had no evidence of her knowing anything beyond the silliest prattle, and there is the sad irony of Clyde's having been so deluded. But Dreiser's presentation of Sondra is not primarily satirical. He was trying to suggest the social set in its animation as well as its superficiality, and for this he had none of the equipment that was second nature to Scott Fitzgerald. Both words and tune seem wrong this time, and not merely when Sondra coos: "Cantum be happy out here wis Sonda and all these nicey good-baddies?" When Gilbert says, "Spin the big news, Dad," or one of the college boys asks, "Did you hear who is being touted for stroke next year over at Cornell?" we have no illusion that we are listening to possible talk.

The third book, consisting entirely of the trial and its aftermath, raises the chief questions about structure. Dreiser devotes over a hundred thousand words to the account of the trial itself, from the first introduction of the local coroner, leafing through a mail-order catalogue when the telephone rings, to the verdict of guilty. Here the novel becomes documentary in the most literal sense. Many of the lawyers' speeches are based very closely upon what was actually said, and even Roberta's pathetic letters to Clyde, which become the most affecting evidence against him, often reproduce almost verbatim those of Grace Brown. The question, as in all such matters, is what Dreiser made of his sources, and here opinion has been very divided. For some readers interest breaks down under the sheer weight of details; for others the exhaustiveness of Dreiser's treatment is what builds up to an effect of final authority. Eisenstein, for instance, admired the whole novel for being "as broad and shoreless as the Hudson . . . as immense as life itself," and regarded it in its total structure as an "epic of cosmic veracity and objectivity."

It is certainly the most carefully planned of all Dreiser's novels, and though its movement is slow, it advances magisterially from beginning to end. He made use of a simple but effective "framing" device to suggest the bounds of Clyde's world, virtually duplicating his opening and closing chapters. In each he takes us into the deep canyon of a big city on a languorous summer night, and shows us the Griffiths family group lifting their voices in song "against the vast scepticism and apathy of life." He could hardly have produced a more concentrated impression of the overpowering and dwarfing metropolitan desert—of "such walls," as he remarks parenthetically, "as in time may linger as a mere fable." They are no fable here. They are the stone and steel of Kansas City at the beginning, and of San Francisco at the end. But at the end Clyde's place has been taken by Esta's boy, now eight years old.

Dreiser also introduced a few more developed devices of foreshadowing than he had tried before. For example, when Clyde first meets Roberta outside the factory, he invites her out in an amusement park boat, and she asks "Will it be perfectly safe?" Thus is she launched upon the utter insecurity of her relationship with him which will end only when, at a far more distant and deserted spot, she will step down into the boat of her death. A comparable way of causing us to look back to the start is the parting gift to Clyde from another man in the death house, a lawyer who, though a refined intellectual in looks and manner, has been convicted of poisoning an old man of great wealth. He leaves Clyde his copy of *The Arabian Nights*.

But such thematic devices are still sparse in Dreiser's method, and he depends for his dramatic effects primarily upon the kind of bare contrasts he had used in *Sister Carrie*. One of the strongest of these also bears out how, despite the great length of this novel, many of the individual scenes are very compact. In a chapter of only three pages he affords us two glimpses, first by Roberta of Clyde's world, and then by him of hers. Anguished now by the thought that he is going to desert her, Roberta comes along Central Avenue to see him standing beside the car of one of Sondra's friends, and the girl "affectedly posed at the wheel" is for Roberta "an epitome of all the security, luxury, and freedom from responsibility" which are enticing Clyde away. Put side by side with this is Clyde, riding with his new friends, and getting out of the car to ask directions at a farmhouse. He momentarily stops short in his tracks, and Sondra calls, "What's the matter, Clyde? Afraid of the bow-wow?" He has read the name on the mailbox, Titus Alden, and here in this dilapidated and miserable house, and in the threadbare and beaten figure of the man who he knows must be Roberta's father, he sees the typification of everything that he has most wanted to escape, and that now seems to be extending "its gloomy, poverty-stricken arms" to seize him once more. In both these glimpses, incidentally, clothes still play a central symbolical role.

When one moves from smaller to larger scenes, one gets an increasing sense of the rightness of Dreiser's over-all proportions. The quality of spacing is what makes most memorable a kind of effect he had not attempted before, the suggestion of the remoteness from human contact of the lake to which Clyde lures Roberta. He evokes the desolateness of the spot partly by the very slowness with which he takes the two from their secret meeting in Utica to a pleasant resort, and then to a more remote one, and then to Big Bittern. To heighten its unearthly quality he draws also upon the language of fantasy. Clyde has been compelled here as though "some Giant Efrit" had sprung up in his brain. The water itself is "like a huge, black pearl cast by some

mighty hand, in anger possibly." Some of these details may seem
stock in themselves, but their cumulative effect is to remove
Clyde farther and farther from his charted paths of ordinary
reality, to numb his mind to the point where Roberta becomes to
him "an almost nebulous figure" in "an insubstantial rowboat
upon a purely ideational lake." In this way Dreiser builds up our
acceptance of the involuntary nature of the catastrophe.

But the large questions still remain: wherein is this novel particularly American, and wherein is it a tragedy? Ten years after
the book's appearance, when a boy named Robert Edwards killed
a girl in circumstances running closely parallel to those Dreiser
had treated, he was asked to be a special reporter at the trial. He
also wrote how he had first reached the conclusion that he had
found in such a case "the real American tragedy." He went
back to his newspaper days when he had begun to observe the
consuming passion of his time to be the desire for wealth. He recalled how, furthermore, "pride and show, and even waste, were
flaunted in a new and still fairly virgin land—in the face of
poverty and want not on the part of those who would not work,
but the poverty and want of those who were all too eager to
work, and almost on any terms." In the light of such facts he had
come to believe that the case of Clyde Griffiths was a typical result
of the fierce competitive spirit. He now reaffirmed how not only
typical but also approved by all the standard *mores* was Clyde's
longing to rise.

In the novel itself he had made other generalizations about
America. In dwelling upon Clyde's and Roberta's ignorant lack
of preparation for life, he had observed how both their families
in their unthinking narrow moralism were "excellent examples of
that native type of Americanism which resists facts and reveres
illusion." Incidentally, he introduced a new source to which such
a boy and girl would turn for their standards of judgment and
taste. Clyde, casting around for any means to escape Roberta,
recalls a fake wedding he had seen in a movie. Roberta, looking
forward to their marriage, is pathetically determined to have the
same kind of taffeta afternoon dress that a screen heroine has
worn.

In studying the lines of demarcation and stratification in
Lycurgus, Dreiser is aware that they are hardly peculiar to
America, but he wants to give his particular American facts to
the full, and even notes—though it is not central to his purpose
—how the native girls in the factory hold themselves aloof from

the foreign-born. In his documentation of the trial he emphasizes how the question of Clyde's guilt or innocence becomes a mere incident in the struggle between rival politicians. The Republican District Attorney is also currently a candidate for Judge, so it is natural for Clyde's Democratic lawyers to oppose him by every means they can.

Many other such details could be cited. European observers were to comment upon the restlessness and uprootedness of Clyde's life in contrast to the more fixed patterns that still prevailed among them, as also upon the absence of any traditional culture even in the upper class. But Dreiser's central thought in putting the word American into his title was the overwhelming lure of money-values in our society, more nakedly apparent than in older and more complex social structures. And just as the flame was more bright and compelling, so were its victims drawn to it more helplessly.

But are such victims figures for tragedy? There has hardly ever been a more unheroic hero than Clyde, and Dreiser did everything he could not to build him up. He is good-looking, to be sure, with his black hair and white skin and nice smile, and with a wistfully appealing quality that makes him superficially attractive—indeed, not unlike a minor movie hero. But Dreiser keeps repeating that he is essentially selfish, with no steadily deep feelings for others, and with no serious consideration for Roberta in her trouble. Dreiser tells us near the beginning that Clyde, over-impressed by every sign of wealth, revealed "a soul that was not destined to grow up." As he moves into the final debate with himself over what to do about Roberta, his weak and scattered mind is never able to face the real facts. He shows no trace of greater maturity at this time of crisis.

As Clyde plots murder in spite of himself, Dreiser goes to the opposite extreme from the writer of a detective story. Everything that Clyde does is so inept that he is discovered at once. He plans nothing straight and leaves every kind of clue in his wake, even letters in the trunk at his rooming house that spell out the whole situation. These he had kept out of "an insane desire" for anything that showed "a kindness, a tenderness toward him." No wonder the prosecution regards him as possessing only "the most feeble and blundering incapacity." And he is hardly more than a puppet in his own attorneys' hands as he sits listening to the line of defense in which they coach him. They know that they can do nothing with the unlikely truth of the acidental killing without dressing it up. They present him as "a mental and moral coward," who underwent "a change of heart" towards Roberta, and decided to marry her after all. He recites this lie by rote. The charged hostility of the unbelieving courtroom is relieved by "the solemn vengeful voice" of a woodsman: "Why don't they kill the God-damned bastard and be done with him?"

Yet Dreiser does not mean us to share in this judgment, and we do not, despite the immense problem he faced in creating any sympathy for such a pawn. Earlier American writers had dealt with the theme of young men driven to murder by forces stronger than themselves, but their emphases had been very different. Hawthorne's Donatello, in boyish devotion to Miriam, acted in sudden unthinking frenzy to free her from the sinister figure who shadowed her. Melville's Billy Budd, horrified by the falseness of the accusation that he had been plotting mutiny, hit out instinctively, and (as Captain Vere said) it is as though Claggart were "struck dead by an angel of God." James's Hyacinth Robinson, caught between the conflicting claims of his devotion to the Princess Casamassima and the commands of the political underground to perform a revolutionary murder, cannot support the tension, and chooses suicide instead. In each case the study is one of essential innocence, and the weakness of a Hyacinth Robinson is not enough to interfere with our feeling for him.

But Dreiser had gone farther even than Melville in his questioning of free will. In presenting Clyde he gave the most complete illustration of his belief that "the essential tragedy of life" is that man is "a waif and an interloper in Nature," which desires only "to work through him," and that he has "no power to make his own way." He can lead us to respond to Clyde's situation only to the extent that we follow the defense attorney's description of him as "a mental and moral coward" into the further statement: "Not that I am condemning you for anything that you cannot help. After all, you didn't make yourself, did you?" This is the same expression Dreiser had used in *The Hand of the Potter*. One of Clyde's last fumbling reflections in the death house returns again to the essential point: "Would no one ever understand—or give him credit for his human—if all too human and perhaps wrong hungers—yet from which so many others—along with himself suffered?" Powys said of Dreiser: "No man I ever met is so sympathetic with weakness." A crucial element in our final estimate of this novel is how far he can enable us to participate in his compassion.

He has deprived himself of many of the most powerful attributes of traditional tragedy. Rejecting the nineteenth-century myth of the free individual, which his experience has proved to him to be false, he has now gone to the opposite pole in portraying an individual without any purposive will. He has decided that a situation like Clyde's was far more widely typical of America than one like Cowperwood's. But if in a sense Cowperwood was above tragedy, Clyde is below it, since there can be no real drama without conflict. In *Pierre* Melville had made his most devastating critique of optimistic individualism. But caught by his own despair he had also presented a young character so dominated by fate that we do not have the catharsis that can come only out of some mature struggle against doom. Dreiser is not despairing in *An American Tragedy*. He is writing with objective detachment. But as is the case in most of O'Neill's plays, he sees man so exclusively as the overwhelmed victim that we feel hardly any of the crisis of moral guilt that is also at the heart of the tragic experience.

But in considering the final effect of the novel we must not fail to reckon with the several chapters after the trial. For here, as he deals with the long months of waiting in the brutal death house, he makes a detailed study of the religious appeals held out to Clyde by his mother and by a young evangelistic minister. Dreiser describes Mrs. Griffiths as "a figure out of the early Biblical days of her six-thousand-year-old world," and really conveys her as such in her square-shouldered if anguished trust in her son, even after his conviction, and in her unwavering if defeated effort to secure his pardon. It may come as more of a surprise that Dreiser speaks of the Reverend Mr. McMillan as a present-day Saint Bernard or Savonarola: "a strange, strong, tense, confused, merciful, and too, after his fashion beautiful soul; sorrowing with misery, yearning toward an impossible justice."

Here the qualifications that clog the prose are also a chief source of Dreiser's strength. To a greater extent even than in his earlier books he was determined to hold on with unrelaxed tenacity until he had given the full record, and he did not want his own unbelief to reduce his preacher to a satirized stereotype. The effect of the Reverend Mr. McMillan's efforts to bring consolation to Clyde is, to be sure, ironic. For as he gains the young man's confidence and hears his whole story, he comes to the saddened conclusion that, though Clyde may be technically innocent on legal grounds, his whole tangled train of thoughts and actions makes him deeply guilty in the eyes of God. But he does not turn against Clyde, but labors to bring him to contrition and conversion. He thinks that he has succeeded. But though Clyde, under his prompting, signs a statement to that effect, as he walks to the electric chair he is not at all sure that he really believes. Nor has there been any of the final recognition of his destiny that frees a Hamlet or a Raskolnikov. Clyde is still a cornered animal.

The street scene of the epilogue, paralleling that of the prologue, makes some small but important thematic additions. The father, who has played such a dim part in Clyde's life, looks even more ineffectual than before. The mother is still the one figure in the group who radiates a preserving if blind trust in divine providence, but her face is now "seamed with lines of misery." When her little grandson, "unsoiled and unspoiled and uncomprehending"—and paying no attention to the service—asks her for a dime to buy an ice-cream cone, she gives it to him thinking of Clyde, thinking that she must be "more liberal" with this boy, and not try to restrain him too much. But essentially she has learned nothing, and the whole course of events might easily be repeated. We feel "the vast scepticism and apathy of life" with greatly increased pressure. Dreiser has not shaped a tragedy in any of the traditional uses of the term, and yet he has written out of a profoundly tragic sense of man's fate. He has made us hear, with more and more cumulative power, the "disastrous beating" of the Furies' wings.

This distinction between tragedy and a tragic sense was not made by the reader who saw this novel most nearly with Dreiser's own eyes. Clarence Darrow read it with complete intensity, moved most by Dreiser's "fanatical devotion to truth," and he felt at the end that he had been "gripped in the hands" of such "a master of tragedy . . . as the world has seldom known." He also said: "Of course my philosophy is practically the same as yours." This kinship between Dreiser and Darrow may help us to define a little more thoroughly what it was that *An American Tragedy* brought to articulation out of our life, and what its significance is in the drift of our cultural history.

The philosophy that these two men shared had, of course, been Darrow's before it was Dreiser's. He was fourteen years the senior, also a product of the Middle West, where he likewise experienced poverty and inferior schooling. But his father was the village agnostic of Kinsman, Ohio, well read in Jefferson, Voltaire, and Paine. By the time therefore that Darrow managed to have a year in the Michigan Law School, his mind was already grounded in a firm rationalism such as Dreiser never knew. One of his major experiences was reading Altgeld's *Our Penal Code and Its Victims* (1884), with its compelling demonstration that the poor man does not receive equal justice. The connecting strand in all his various defenses that brought him to national prominence was his conviction that the criminal is not a free agent.

Darrow's final views, as expressed in *The Story of My Life* (1932), are extraordinarily akin to the burden of *An American Tragedy*. They bear out from a different angle why minds growing to maturity in the late nineteenth century felt such a break with earlier American tradition. Faced with the gross inequalities of Chicago financial life, Darrow came to doubt the doctrine of natural rights expressed by his father's eighteenth-century philosophers. He was to go much farther than that in casting off all traditional sanctions, and to regard any belief in a purposive universe as mere delusion. Like Dreiser he could only brood upon the "meaninglessness" of existence.

And yet, no matter how far-reaching his scepticism, like Dreiser he preserved a core of deeply humane values. His chief concern was the same as that in *An American Tragedy:* society's immense fallibility in arriving at justice. He considered crime as a sickness to be cured. When he developed his theory of how the cure might be effected, he again voiced some of Dreiser's most pervasive thoughts: "Most men and women are haunted by poverty, and all are helpless in the clutch of a relentless fate. . . . To prevent burglary the cause must be removed; it can never be done in any other way."

In regarding the victims of the law he too quoted the line about "the hand of the potter." His most condensed conclusion could have served as an epigraph for Dreiser's treatment of Clyde: "I have always felt sympathy for all living things. . . . I have judged none, and therefore condemned none. I believe that I have excused all who are forced to live awhile upon the earth. I am satisfied that they have done their best with what they had."

This close correspondence between the values of the two men makes us more aware of how representative these values are of their times, more aware too of why Dreiser held them. He viewed a society in which the equality whereon alone democratic justice might be based had been destroyed by the oligarchy of wealth. At this point he was not thinking in political terms; he entertained no ideas of how Clyde's world might be changed; he only

contemplated it with somber resignation. Contemplating for ourselves the extreme to which both Darrow and Dreiser had gone in
their scepticism, we are faced with the grave question of how long
positive values can endure only as the aftershine of something
that has been lost. Dreiser began to sense this as the 'twenties
moved into the 'thirties, and he was caught up far more directly
into political thinking than he had ever been before.

In the meantime *An American Tragedy* was his first immediate
popular success, with a sale of twenty-five thousand in its initial
six months, which still left it far below the ranks of a best seller.
It was banned only in Boston. Mencken, who no longer needed
to be Dreiser's champion, summed up the consensus of favorable
opinion when he said: "Dreiser can feel, and, feeling, he can
move. The others are very skillful with words." Wells agreed
with Bennett that here was "one of the greatest novels of this
century. It is a far more than life-size rendering of a poor little
representative corner of American existence, lighted up by a flash
of miserable tragedy. . . . It gets the large, harsh superficial
truth that it has to tell with a force that no grammatical precision and no correctitude could attain." The word "superficial" is
important to note, particularly as coming from a European. The
shallowness of a Clyde prevents his history from ever reaching the
transfiguration that Dostoevsky dwells upon in the closing pages
of *Crime and Punishment*.

But the thoroughness of Dreiser's treatment, the realization
we have at the end that his mind has moved inexhaustibly, relentlessly over every relevant detail raises the book to the stature
that made Joseph Wood Krutch speak of it as "the great American novel of our generation." There were still many dissenting
voices. Clyde's whole experience was too undifferentiated, too
unilluminated to compel the attention of some readers already
habituated to the masterpieces of the modern psychological novel.
But for young men growing up in the 'twenties and 'thirties here
was a basic account of the world to which they were exposed.

Ellen Moers

Clyde Griffiths:
"The Mechanism Called Man"

> Under the arc lights,
> In the twilight . . .
> With eager, awkward gestures
> And seeking eyes . . .
> It is Main Street . . .
> —THEODORE DREISER, "Links"

Ten years before the publication of *An American Tragedy*, Dreiser went back to the Indiana of his boyhood years to collect impressions for *A Hoosier Holiday*, a work of nostalgic travelogue mixed with autobiography. This return to the Midwest was as important to *An American Tragedy* as the Maumee summer of 1899 had been to *Sister Carrie*, but in a different way. For in 1915 Dreiser re-encountered not only the general spirit of the Midwest (which for him filled the air over Indiana, western Ohio, and Chicago) but the exact scenes of his own birth and youth. He wrote of his excitement upon re-entering Terre Haute, the town where he was born and which he had left as a child of seven or eight and never seen again until now. He found the town still full of the "young, hopeful seeking atmosphere" he remembered: "that something which I have always noticed about American cities and missed abroad . . . a crude, sweet illusion about the importance of all things material."

Though it was no longer the best hotel in town, Dreiser insisted on staying at the Terre Haute House, center of "the seeking life" of the town when he was a boy. The hotel made him think of the symbolic role of such institutions in American life: each city had to have "our largest" hotel, with its imitation onyx lobby, its barber shop and grill room, its porters and bellboys, "all braids and buttons," whose chief duty was to extract tips "from the unwilling and yet ecstatic visitor." He thought of the rich Americans who went to such hotels, the "feverish hunger" in their faces, and the eyes: "The blaze of their skins and eyes! The hardy, animal implications of their eyes!"

Dreiser also thought of "the incomplete, the botched, the semi-articulate" people who never had the chance to go to such hotels; and, still in connection with the Terre Haute House, he thought of his own family, for the hotel awakened old memories. There, in the best of times, his brother Paul had been feted as author of "On the Banks of the Wabash," and, in the worst of times, his mother had worked as a cleaning woman. He remembered the sound of his father's voice, shouting in anger, and he remembered the place of the hotel in the life of his brother Rome.

> For here, once upon a time, my brother Rome, at that time a seeking boy like any of those we now saw pouring up and down this well lighted street—(up and down, up and down, day after day, like those poor moths we see about the lamp)—was in the habit of coming, and, as my father described it, in his best suit of clothes and his best shoes, a toothpick in his mouth, standing in or near the doorway of the hotel, to give the impression that he had just dined there.
>   "Loafers! Idle, good-for-nothings!" I can hear my father exclaiming even now.
>   Yet he was not a loafer by any means—just a hungry, thirsty, curious boy. . . .[1]

There, among the "seeking boys" of Terre Haute, as much as in the records of the Gillette case, Dreiser found Clyde Griffiths, moving up and down, up and down, like the moth before the lamp.

Clyde Griffiths is Dreiser's mature and masterly characterization of the seeking boy. That is all there is to Clyde, but it is a great deal: he is the Everyman of desire. A poor, simple boy who pursues neither honor nor glory nor distinction, Clyde goes doggedly after the goals clearly set in his path by his society, and no farther from him than the nose on his face: pretty girls, nice clothes, sweet foods, good times, and the money and leisure to procure them. Dreiser makes a bitter point of the tawdriness of Clyde's wants:

> evening suit, dress shirt, high hat, bow tie, white kid gloves and patent leather shoes, a costume which at that time Clyde felt to be

---

[1] Theodore Dreiser, *Hoosier Holiday*, pp. 393-99.

the last word in all true distinction, beauty, gallantry and bliss.
To be able to wear such a suit . . . ! To be able to talk to a
girl . . . ! What a true measure of achievement!

But the force of Clyde's desire, as Dreiser says in the same passage, has "all the luster and wonder of a spiritual transfiguration."[2]

Unlike Sister Carrie, who has the capacity for a miraculous
flowering, Clyde is a static, sterile creature incapable of growth.
Responsive to the infinitesimal, attractive stimulus that passes
before it arrives, he also seems incapable of pleasure—to say
nothing (as this novel says nothing) of love. Carrie's womanliness
is rooted lilylike in the mud of country pools, but Clyde has no
natural roots, almost no body. His world is never the natural
one, always the urban and artificial.

It is difficult to imagine Clyde running, jumping, or playing
ball like a normal boy, but he does, of course, have to swim and
row; otherwise he would not be able to begin his seduction of
Roberta Alden on one lake or end her life on another. But from
Clyde's first appearance on the water, in the central section of the
novel, it is clear that these are unnatural accomplishments de-
vised as props to a fantasy life: he acquires them "because he
was always thinking that if by chance he should be taken up by
the Griffiths, he would need as many social accomplishments as
possible. . . ."

One lovely summer afternoon, Clyde goes rowing on Crum
Lake. He feels no immediate, physical pleasure. Instead, "his mind
indulged itself in day dreams as to how it would feel to be a member of one of the wealthy groups that frequented one of the more
noted resorts of the north. . . ." The lapse into society-column
and advertising clichés is typical of Clyde: tree-rimmed Crum
Lake dissolves before his hungry eyes into "the shores of a scene
more distingué than this." And the boat itself, sliding softly
through the water, becomes another dream: "might he not be
. . . racing from place to place in some high-powered car, Sondra
by his side?"[3] The automobile, weapon of the hit-and-run accident that brings to a close the first book of the novel, signifies
many things in *An American Tragedy:* wealth, speed, rootlessness, sexual object, social menace. But it is quintessentially the
antinatural thing.

---

[2] *An American Tragedy* (New York: Dell, The Laurel Dreiser, 1960), I,
iv, 41-42 (hereafter *AAT*).
[3] *AAT,* II, vi, 278-80.

We see the outside world through Clyde's "seeking eyes" as a series of highly tinted, patently fake images—the sort that appear on picture post cards or travel folders, or in the rotogravure pages of the newspapers. There is also Clyde's wintery glimpse of posh Wykeagy Avenue in Lycurgus, where lights gleaming through falling snow "gave it a Christmas-card effect." Just before the murder, Clyde has his chance at last to go to fashionable Twelfth Lake, where Sondra and all her showy friends have their summer homes. This is the way Twelfth Lake, for which he has yearned so hard and so long, looks to Clyde:

> And then this scene, where a bright sun poured a flood of crystal light upon a greensward that stretched from tall pines to the silver rippling waters of a lake. And off shore . . . the bright white sails of small boats—the white and green and yellow splashes of color, where canoes paddled by idling lovers were passing in the sun! Summertime—leisure—warmth—color—ease—beauty—love[4]

—everything but reality.

The thoughts that pass through Clyde's mind take up, at a guess, about half the wordage of Dreiser's long novel. Yet what these words essentially establish is the thinness, the accidental indefiniteness of Clyde's consciousness. He is always thinking the same thing: "*I want*"—with its variations (I want—I shouldn't want—I want very badly—I must find a way to get—I'm afraid I won't get—I want anyway). He understands little; he rarely reflects; certainly he says nothing worth listening to.

In Clyde's speech, the word that concentrates all the force of his wanting, in all its stupidity, is "Gee!" He may get a job in a big fancy hotel: "Gee! what would that mean?" (It means "a good time, gee!") Against the claims of pride, of which he has little, and the voice of reason, which he does not hear, Clyde pursues a vulgar, calculating tease of a shopgirl:

> And as he saw her order whatever she liked, without any thought of his purse, he contemplated quickly her face, figure, the shape of her hands . . . the swell of her bust . . . the curve of her eyebrows, the rounded appeal of her smooth cheeks and chin. There was something also about the tone of her voice, unctuous, smooth, which somehow appealed to and disturbed him. To him it was delicious. Gee, if he could only have such a girl all for himself![5]

[4] *AAT,* II, xxv, 342; xliii, 477.
[5] *AAT,* I, iv, 48; v, 53; xii, 99-100.

A polite "Gee!" serves Clyde in his courtship of a country girl ("Hello. Gee, it's nice to have you meet me"); a more intense "Gee, I'm wild!" in that of a sophisticated debutante. Whether in awe, in terror, in delight, or in dismay at the causes and consequences of desire, the same cry rises to Clyde's lips. It expresses all his consciousness of being on trial for his life, and being exposed by witnesses to his crime: "Gee!—he was going to tell about that now, maybe." And when at last he is condemned as a murderer, and his mother stands before Clyde in the death house (her heavy body heaving with sobs, her broad back turned away to hide her tears, her fingers fumbling for a handkerchief, her lips muttering "My God—why hast Thou forsaken me?"), Clyde has still no more than this to set as seal on his own tragedy: "But you mustn't, Ma. Gee, you mustn't cry."[6]

Clyde Griffiths, in other words, is that statistical wretch, the inexplicable, unsympathetic delinquent. (Darken his skin and his crime, and he becomes the model, as in fact he was, for Richard Wright's *Native Son*.) Dreiser does not pretend either to explain or to like Clyde, but he is true to him—and most true when he protects the banality of Clyde's response to life from incursions of poetry, sentiment, or idealism. This kind of truth was Dreiser's particular contribution to the art of realism, and he had begun to practice it in *Sister Carrie*. But it was one thing to center a novel on an inarticulate character who is also a pretty and charming young girl; and quite another thing to make a hero out of a boy who kills a pretty and charming young girl and then says "Gee!"

Nevertheless, Clyde's role in *An American Tragedy* must be described as that of the hero, oddly as the word seems to suit the quality of his mind and the nature of his end. When the cap is at last fixed on Clyde's head, the straps adjusted, and the current turned on, something enormously important comes to a stop: a seeking life. The pity and terror aroused by Clyde at the end, and indeed throughout the novel, are augmented, not diminished, by the minimally human level of his existence. The final achievement of Dreiser's naturalism was his celebration of the precious, the tragic significance of man as mechanism.

Without words, then, and almost without physical weight, Clyde must press heavily on the world inside the novel (and out-

---

[6] *AAT*, II, xvii, 297; xxxii, 394; III, xix, 677; xxix, 808.

side it—for the reader is never free from the pressure of his need). Dreiser accomplished this through his control of what Robert Penn Warren has called "the movie in our heads"—that is, a shift of focus which, as Warren writes, "is never arbitrary; it grows out of the expressive needs of the narrative as Dreiser has conceived it, and out of the prior fact that the narrative is conceived in a drama between the individual and the universe." Where the individual Clyde is concerned, at every important twist of the narrative Dreiser gives us a "closeup" of Clyde's face; and in that face it is the eyes that speak better than the mouth the tale of Clyde's desire.

This camera-like technique undoubtedly derived from Dreiser's fascination with the film, which began in the early 1920s when he was working on the *Tragedy* in or near Hollywood and listening to Helen's experiences of making movies.[7] But the extraordinary role played by Clyde's eyes in the novel also came out of Dreiser's program as a mechanist. The look in Clyde's "seeking eyes" is the perpetual sign of his response to environmental stimulus—and also the *means* of that response. The eyes make things happen; they make Clyde what he is. Compelling and convincing, these eyes make other characters in the novel act on his behalf—and keep us, the readers, from asking awkward questions about consciousness and will that Dreiser will not answer. The eyes of Clyde involve us in his fate with a sense of discomfort and alarm that nothing in his character can explain.

In the first chapter of the novel an unnamed boy of twelve comes into view as part of a family group wandering the downtown streets of an unnamed city. Dreiser gives here virtually all the physical description he will ever give of Clyde: a silhouette in black and white.

> The boy moved restlessly from one foot to the other, keeping his eyes down. . . . A tall and as yet slight figure, surmounted by an interesting head and face—white skin, dark hair—he seemed more keenly observant and decidedly more sensitive than most of the others—appeared indeed to resent and even to suffer from the position in which he found himself.

Dreiser keeps Clyde's eyes down, averted from the reader throughout the introductory scene, for desire has not yet come to him,

---

[7] Robert Penn Warren, *"An American Tragedy," Yale Review,* October 1962, pp. 8-9; Helen Dreiser, *Dreiser,* Chapter 5; for Dreiser's lasting interest in the technique of the film, see Marguerite Tjader, *Dreiser,* pp. 52-56.

only resentment. But the power of Clyde's look to "interest" and to "seem" and to "appear" is already established. The crowd responds:

> "That oldest boy don't wanta be here. He feels outa place, I can see that. . . ."
> "Yeh, I guess that's so," the other assented, taking in the peculiar cast of the boy's head and face . . . the uneasy and self-conscious expression upon the face whenever it was lifted.[8]

As Clyde's independent life begins, he looks into the mirror at this face: ". . . . not so bad-looking—a straight, well-cut nose, high white forehead, wavy, glossy, black hair, eyes that were black and rather melancholy at times." At sixteen, Clyde decides to find a good job, something superior to the ill-paying odd chores he has done as a boy. He approaches the cashier of the city's leading drugstore. "Interested by his tentative and uncertain manner, as well as his deep and rather appealing eyes," she sends him on to the manager, an irritable fellow who normally would not give a job-seeker the time of day. But "Clyde cast at him a glance that said as plain as anything could, 'If you have any such place, I wish you would please give it to me. I need it.'" The manager tries to turn away, "but seeing a flicker of disappointment and depression pass over Clyde's face," he pauses instead to tell Clyde to go further, on to the bell-captain of the Green-Davidson hotel, the best hotel in town.[9] This is Clyde's first chance.

At the hotel, Clyde wins the necessary protection of the most experienced of his fellow bellboys, "more because of the way he looked and inquired and listened than because of anything Clyde did or said." At the brothel to which they take him, a prostitute —first of the women of the novel to respond to Clyde—responds to the look on his face.

> "You haven't been working over at the hotel very long, have you?"
> "No," said Clyde, a little irritated by this, his eyebrows and the skin of his forehead rising and falling as he talked—a form of contraction and expansion that went on involuntarily whenever he was nervous or thought deeply. . . .
> "I just knew you hadn't. You don't look very much like these other boys—you look different." She smiled. . . . "I like you.

---

[8] *AAT*, I, i, 21, 23.
[9] *AAT*, I, ii, 31; iv, 44-45.

. . . I like your eyes. You're not like those other fellows. You're more refined, kinda. I can tell. . . ."

"Oh, I don't know," replied Clyde, very much pleased and flattered, his forehead wrinkling and clearing as before.[10]

This facial mannerism, a frame to Clyde's expressive eyes, will often reappear in the novel. It is as involuntary—that is, as mechanical—as the responses of the prostitute.

Clyde's hotel life is abruptly shattered at the end of Book I. A night of pleasure with his bellboy friends ends in a wild car ride back to the hotel. The car has been "borrowed"; there is an accident; a little girl is killed; and Clyde runs away from job, home, city, childhood. When we meet Clyde again, at the beginning of Book II, three years have passed and we see "a modified version" of Clyde: "now twenty, a little taller and more firmly but scarcely any more robustly built." He is still a bellboy, but now working at the Union League Club in Chicago.

Samuel Griffiths, Clyde's rich uncle from Lycurgus, New York, comes to the club on a business trip. Clyde has never met the man, but he has heard of his money and his shirt factory—where there might be a job for Clyde. Again a chance for Clyde, and an even more important one. He introduces himself to his uncle, makes a few winning speeches—but it is not so much what Clyde says as the way he looks that affects Samuel Griffiths: "he paused, smiling, and yet with an inquiring look in his eye. His uncle looked solemnly at him for a moment, pleased by his looks and his general manner of approach." What Griffiths sees is a family resemblance to Clyde's father, which arouses conflicting emotions of guilt and distaste; yet there is a difference. For Samuel's brother, at the same age, had been "a bit mushy," while Clyde appears alert, intelligent, and ambitious. The yearning look in Clyde's eyes flatters the older man: "plainly he and his achievements had stood in the nature of an ideal to this youth."[11]

Clyde is offered a job in the Griffiths factory and moves to Lycurgus. But the job turns out to be trivial and poorly paid, and for a long time Clyde is given no reason to expect admission to the charmed circle of Griffiths wealth and respectability. But at long last Clyde is invited to his uncle's home—another chance, another crisis. As Clyde enters the Griffiths mansion, the father stands hesitant, the mother cold, the brother—an oddly exact

---

[10] *AAT*, I, ix, 77; x, 82-83.
[11] *AAT*, II, iii, 178; iv, 191-94.

physical copy of Clyde, in all but the eyes—openly hostile. But one of the Griffiths daughters, the homely one, makes Clyde welcome because "there was something, as she now saw, about Clyde's eyes—nervous and somewhat furtive and appealing or seeking—that at once interested her, and reminded her, perhaps, since she was not much of a success socially either, of something in herself."[12]

The story of Clyde's sexual triumphs makes Book II a whirling, flashing dance of looks and eyes, which Dreiser introduces with a joke. Clyde meets two girls at a church social, who take him home for an evening of dancing, promise of social and sexual fulfillment to come; the first record they dance to is called "Brown Eyes." (The second, a somewhat less pleasant joke, is "The Love Boat.")[13]

Clyde's conquest of Roberta Alden, the country girl who comes to work in his department at the factory, begins with the "darkness and melancholy and lure of his eyes." It culminates in a seduction scene—if that is the right word for a scene of threat and terror—which is remarkedly different in tone from the parallel scene in *Sister Carrie*. Dreiser had filled his account of Carrie's seduction with warmth and sunshine, with the sense of youth and growth, but in the *Tragedy* Roberta's seduction takes place outside nature and close to death, although (perhaps because) Dreiser makes the scene far more overtly sexual in suggestion.

Here Dreiser completes the desubstantiation of Clyde that has been becoming ever more apparent and increasingly ominous throughout the central section of the novel. Clyde is reduced to a look and a shadow, his body dismembered, his eyes turned black, opaquely hard, inhuman. Roberta cries out:

"I can't, Clyde, I can't. I would if I could but I can't. It wouldn't be right. I would if I could make myself, but I can't."

She looked up into his face, a pale oval in the dark, trying to see if he would not see, sympathize, be moved in her favor. However, irritated by this plainly definite refusal, he was not now to be moved. . . .

At once, and with an irritated shrug of the shoulders, as she now saw, he turned and started to leave her. . . .

"Please don't go, Clyde. Please don't leave me. . . ."

With a twist he released his body from her arm and started walking briskly down the street in the dark.

---

[12] *AAT*, II, ix, 238.
[13] *AAT*, II, viii, 226-27.

And Roberta, stricken . . . called, "Clyde!" And then ran after him a little way. . . . But he did not return. Instead he went briskly on. . . . Her Clyde! And she started running in his direction a little, but as suddenly stopped. . . . For on the one hand all her conventional training was now urging her to stand firm . . . whereas on the other, all her desires . . . urged her to run after him before it was too late, and he was gone. His beautiful face, his beautiful hands. His eyes. And still the receding echo of his feet. . . .

And he was already out of hearing, walking briskly and grimly on, the click and echo of his receding steps falling less and less clearly on her suffering ears.

It was the first flashing, blinding, bleeding stab of love for her.

The seduction is completed the next morning at the factory. Roberta and Clyde search out and avoid each other with their eyes. Finally Roberta writes Clyde a note and, passing by his desk, drops it into his hands.

He looked up instantly, his dark eyes still hard at the moment with the mingled pain and unrest and dissatisfaction and determination . . . and noting Roberta's retreating figure as well as the note he at once relaxed. . . . He opened it and read. And as instantly his body was suffused with a warm and yet very weakening ray.

And Roberta in turn . . . now looked cautiously about, a strained and nervous look in her eyes. But seeing Clyde looking directly at her, his eyes filled with a conquering and yet yielding light and a smile upon his lips, and his head nodding a happy assent, she as suddenly experienced a dizzying sensation, as though her hitherto constricted blood, detained by a constricted heart and constricted nerves, were as suddenly set free. And all the dry marshes and cracked and parched banks of her soul—the dry rivulets and streams and lakes of misery that seemed to dot her being—were as instantly flooded with this rich upwelling force of life and love.

He would meet her. They would meet tonight. He would put his arms around her and kiss her as before. She would be able to look into his eyes. . . .[14]

Clyde's conquest of Sondra Finchley, the most glamorous Lycurgus debutante, runs parallel with that of Roberta, but it begins in "a closed car of great size and solidity." Mistaking him for his

---

[14] *AAT,* II, xiv, 276; xx, 317-18; xxi, 324.

cousin Gilbert, whom she knows and does not like, Sondra offers Clyde a lift and then, alone with him in the car,

> leaned back after the best princess fashion, her glance examining Clyde's very regular features with interest. He had such soft smiling eyes she thought. . . . She saw that he was nervous and bashful. . . . There was an admiring, pleading light in his eyes which now quite charmed her. What a pleasing young man—so different to Gilbert . . . what would Gilbert think . . . how angry he would be. . . . The thought had a most pleasing tang for her.

That Clyde should be successful with Sondra is inherently improbable, for, quite apart from the matter of his temperamental weaknesses, Clyde is too poor and unsophisticated to pass as smoothly as he seems to do into Sondra's world of flappers and college "grads." But at the center of the novel Dreiser loses interest in probabilities; he establishes, on the contrary, the growing unreality of Clyde's world. The pretty, sexy girls cut to a pattern; the shiny cars; the college songs, and slang and dance rhythms; the confusingly overlapping parties and sporting events; the nauseating witchery of Sondra's baby talk, running like mockery through the social whirl: all these make paradise recede from Clyde's vision as fast as it approaches.

The eyes are still what we have of Clyde, but they have changed beyond recognition. They are no longer soft and melancholy with desire but hard and brilliant with a light that seems to come from a source beyond Clyde. They are black and cold to Roberta; and to Sondra, Clyde's eyes now appear "disturbing," and cast a spell in which fear is an ingredient. They are lit with a "compelling intensity," with a "blazing desire," with "that alluring light which so fascinated her."

On the eve of the murder there is an extraordinary "love scene" between Clyde and Sondra at the lake, when Clyde's eyes become independent objects of enchantment which glow from his disembodied head with a mysterious brilliance.

> "Sondra so glad Clydie here. Misses him so much." She smoothed his hair as he kissed her, and Clyde, bethinking him of the shadow which lay so darkly between them, crushed her feverishly, desperately. "Oh, my darling baby girl . . . I wish I could tell you *all*. I wish I could."
>
> But he could not now—or ever. . . . He would be left, abandoned on the instant, and with what horror in her eyes!

Yet looking into his eyes, his face white and tense, and the glow of the moon above making small white electric sparks in his eyes, she exclaimed . . .

"Does he love Sondra so much? Oh, sweetie boy! Sondra loves him, too." She seized his head between her hands and held it tight, kissing him swiftly and ardently a dozen times. "And Sondra won't give her Clydie up either. . . . It doesn't matter what happens now. . . ."[15]

After "what happens now"—the murder, the trial, and the execution—nothing remains of Clyde but a memory in the mind of the Reverend Duncan McMillan, who has counseled Clyde in his cell, walked with him through the last door, and witnessed the end.

It was the Reverend McMillan, who, gray and weary—a quarter of an hour later, walked desolately . . . through the cold doors of the prison. . . . Dead! He, Clyde, had walked so nervously and yet somehow trustingly beside him but a few minutes before—and now he was dead. The law! . . . That confession! Had he decided truly—with the wisdom of God, as God gave him to see wisdom? Had he? Clyde's eyes! . . .

He walked along the silent street—only to be compelled to pause and lean against a tree—leafless in the winter—so bare and bleak. Clyde's eyes! That look as he sank limply into that terrible chair, his eyes fixed nervously and, as he thought, appealingly and dazedly upon him. . . .[16]

---

[15] *AAT,* II, xxii, 330-33; xxvii, 359, 361; xliii, 478.
[16] *AAT,* III, xxxiv, 859.

William L. Phillips

The Imagery of Dreiser's Novels

For all its apparent concern with the workings of American society and legal machinery, *An American Tragedy* is, with the possible exception of *The "Genius,"* more an "interior" novel than anything which Dreiser had written up to this time. It is documentary, but it documents the internal states of Clyde Griffiths, rather than the risings and fallings of the public fortune of a man like Cowperwood. The symbolic structure of *An American Tragedy* is also significántly different. The conflict which gave *Sister Carrie* and the Cowperwood novels their central unity—the conflict between the seemingly impersonal, inhuman workings of an indifferent universe and the yearning of the individual for a realization of beauty and security—was presented in two opposing sets of images, the universe as a sea or a jungle and the world of dreams as a magic harbor or chamber. Now in *An American Tragedy* the animal imagery becomes so infrequent and diffuse that most of the examples seem to be the result of habit rather than of conscious intent; the few really functional instances are the concentration of references to Clyde as a harried animal in the short time between Roberta's death and his seizure by the agents of the law. Furthermore, the imagery of the sea and the tempest has almost entirely disappeared, or rather has been transformed into the more restricted images of a lake or a pool. What remains constant in Dreiser's imagery is the motif of *The Arabian Nights*. Although one may suspect that the *Arabian Nights* imagery of the early books derived from an unconscious imitation of nineteenth-century pseudo-romances and popular plays, Dreiser in *An American Tragedy* developed it more fully than in any of the earlier novels and used it to provide the central fable of Clyde Griffiths' life. In place of the tension between the actuality of a turbulent sea and the illusion of a secure chamber which provided the central contrast of the earlier novels, Dreiser has in *An American Tragedy* substituted the theme of the

Reprinted from *PMLA*, LXXVIII (December 1963), 580-83, by permission of the Modern Language Association of America. Copyright 1963 by the Modern Language Association of America.

ambiguity of reality, symbolized by the glittering lake which is transformed into a pool of death, and an Aladdin's cave which is transformed into a tomb.

The imagery of *The Arabian Nights* provides the symbolic structure for *An American Tragedy*. Late in Clyde's trial, his defense attorney points to this structure most directly when he speaks of Clyde's attraction to Sondra as "a case of the Arabian Nights, of the ensorcelled and the ensorcellor . . . a case of being bewitched . . . by beauty, love, wealth, by things that we sometimes think we want very, very much, and cannot ever have."[1] Although Clyde does not understand what the lawyer means, and the lawyer himself is merely indulging in rhetoric for the jury, he has provided the key to Dreiser's dominant image of Clyde. Throughout its 800 pages the novel is permeated with the quality of Scheherazade's tales, from the beginning description of Clyde as a twelve-year old boy with "a certain emotionalism and exotic sense of romance" and a "vivid and intelligent imagination" (I, 10) to the end in the death house, where Clyde is given a gift of a copy of *The Arabian Nights* by a man condemned to death "for poisoning an old man of great wealth" (II, 362, 369). Again the language with which Dreiser explores Clyde's personality is less the language of science than the language of romance; "chemisms" are spoken of much less frequently than "dreams," the key word of this novel. Clyde has "wishes," "phantasies," and "visions"; he sees and hears "apparitions," "genii," "effrits," "ghosts," "giants," "ouphes," "barghests," and "ogres"; and he and the other characters are "ensorcelled," "enchanted," "enslaved," "infatuated," "entranced," and "transported" by "witchery" and by dreams which are "mysterious" and "insubstantial," and visions which "materialize."[2]

---

[1] Theodore Dreiser, *An American Tragedy* (2 vols.; New York, 1925), II, 274. Further references to *An American Tragedy* are made to this edition, and will be incorporated into the text. Matthiessen, pp. 194 and 200, briefly treats the *Arabian Nights* theme in the novel. Dreiser's acquaintance with *The Arabian Nights* probably dates from his early childhood, but it was continued in the theaters and music halls of Chicago; see Robert H. Elias, *Theodore Dreiser: Apostle of Nature* (New York, 1949), p. 25. His interest in Eastern legend is to be seen not only in the frequent use of Oriental imagery in his major novels but also in his unfortunate excursions into such pseudo-Oriental tales as "Khat" and "The Prince Who Was a Thief" in *Chains* (New York, 1927).

[2] I, 48, 175, 265, 331, 341, 376; II, 42, 48, 49, 56, 65, 118, 233, 274, 381. References to Clyde's dreams are found in I, 33, 84, 116, 136, 138, 175, 192, 228, 230, 309, 427, 428; II, 5, 16, 27, 31, 50, 133, 221, 229, 383, 385, 392, 405.

More particularly, three stories of *The Arabian Nights* sequence are relevant to the life of Clyde Griffiths—"The History of Aladdin, or the Wonderful Lamp," "The History of the Barber's Fifth Brother," and "The History of the Fisherman." As in *Sister Carrie*, it is the first of these stories which is most frequently mentioned, but here the parallels are more explicit. Like Aladdin, Clyde is a poor boy who disregards the advice of his parents; and like Aladdin, he is conducted into a cavern by a long-lost uncle, who tries to keep him imprisoned until he discovers the magic ring and lamp which provide him wealth, social position, and a beautiful wife. Clyde's imagination is his own genie of the lamp, however. Coupled with his inexperience, it is capable of transforming vulgarity and gaudiness into exotic beauty. When he first visits a house of prostitution, "having pushed through the curtains of heavy velvet . . . Clyde found himself in a bright and rather gaudy parlor or reception room, the walls of which were ornamented with gilt-framed pictures of nude or semi-nude girls and some very high pier mirrors. . . . It was really quite an amazing and Aladdin-like scene to him" (ɪ, 63, 65). The hotel in which he works, however, gauche Dreiser and the reader may find it, is to Clyde a wonder of his world: "[through] a green-marbled doorway . . . he beheld a lobby . . . more arresting, quite, than anything he had seen before. It was all so lavish. Under his feet was a checkered black-and-white marble floor. Above him a coppered and stained and gilded ceiling. And supporting this, a veritable forest of black marble columns as highly polished as the floor— glassy smooth. . . . He gazed about in awe and amazement" (ɪ, 29–30). Later Dreiser carefully poses Clyde at the doorway to the Griffiths factory and then the Griffiths house in an attitude of awe at an excitingly new world (ɪ, 189–190, 219–220), and magically these doors respond to his "Open, Sesame!" It must be remembered that many of Clyde Griffiths' dreams are accomplished. His dreams of a job as bell-boy at the Green-Davidson are fulfilled, and he is ecstatic in his delight: "Kind Heaven! What a realization of paradise! What a consummation of luxury!" (ɪ, 33, 37); each tip is "a mysterious and yet sacred vision" (ɪ, 41). His dream of an outing with Hortense Briggs is made possible by the sudden appearance of a Packard which belonged to "an elderly and very wealthy man who at the time was traveling in Asia" (ɪ, 123). Later in Chicago his uncle, imagined as "a king of Croesus, living in ease and luxury there in the east" (ɪ, 14), suddenly appears at the Chicago Union League Club to offer him a new opportunity just after Clyde had "wished and wished that he could get into some work where he could rise and be somebody" (i, 175). Still later we find Clyde canoeing on Crum Lake, lonely and wishing that Roberta Alden were with him, when she appears on the shore; Clyde's face is "lit by the radiance of one who had suddenly, and beyond his belief, realized a dream," while to Roberta, Clyde is "a pleasant apparition suddenly evoked out of nothing and nowhere, a poetic effort taking form out of smoke or vibrant energy" (i, 265). And finally Clyde, as the result of an accidental meeting at night before the gates of a Wykeagy Avenue palace, is taken up by Sondra Finchley, "a princess" (i, 315), a "goddess in her shrine of gilt and tinsel" (i, 323), "a star, a paragon of luxury and social supremacy" (i, 374), whose glances "enslave" him (i, 315, 323, 341, 374). Some of Clyde's wishes and dreams are indeed "materialized."

The successful Aladdin, however, was only one of the poor youths in *The Arabian Nights* sequence; Alnashar, the Barber's Fifth Brother, is in some respects closer to Clyde Griffiths. Alnashar, it may be remembered, is a lazy, imaginative, and talkative youth who inherits 100 drachms of silver, and invests his inheritance in a stock of bottles and glass objects which he displays for sale on a tray. While waiting for customers he dreams of how he will sell his glasses, reinvest his profits in more glasses, and so on until he has 100,000 drachms, which enable him to dress like a prince, give gifts to the grand vizier, and demand his beautiful daughter as a bride. Then after his marriage he will pretend to lose interest in his bride, and when she and her mother come to plead for his favor, he will push them away violently. At this point Alnashar's dream becomes so real to him that he thrusts out his foot and knocks his tray of glasses to the street, where they lie in fragments. Although Dreiser mentions Alnashar at only one point in the novel (i, 317), he describes Clyde's Alnashar dreams many times: "To be able to wear such a suit with such ease and air! To be able to talk to a girl after the manner and with the sang-froid of some of these gallants! . . . And once he did attain it —was able to wear such clothes as these—well, then was he not well set upon the path that leads to all blisses? . . . The friendly smiles! The secret handclasps, maybe—an arm about the waist of someone or another—a kiss—a promise of marriage—and then, and then!"[3] Furthermore, Clyde is like Alnashar, who continued

---

[3] i, 26. A similar Alnashar dream is stimulated by Sondra Finchley: "Sondra, Twelfth Lake, society, wealth, her love and beauty. He grew not a

to be victimized throughout his life because of his impractical dreaming, in that he never really *learns*. The "dream" just quoted comes when Clyde is fifteen; another, equally Alnashar-like, comes when he is twenty-one. Between the two he has had his dream of securing Hortense Briggs shattered by a discovery of her vulgar self-centeredness, his dream of rising in the hotel business shattered by a procession of unrewarding jobs, his dream of rising rapidly in the Griffiths factory shattered by the drudgery which his relatives prescribe for him, and his dream of having Roberta as lover without any responsibility for her shattered by the discovery of her pregnancy. Critics who emphasize society's responsibility for Clyde's failure forget how really foolish Clyde is. Mason, the district attorney who solves Clyde's murder plot and takes him into custody in less than four days time, contemptuously calls Clyde "a dunce" (II, 150), and Dreiser frequently underlines Clyde's thoughtlessness with phrases like "no thought," "none of the compulsion of the practical," "no serious consideration," "no more plan than this," "he hadn't really thought about that," "he had not even stopped to look," and "he had never thought of them" (II, 5, 8, 17, 61, 129, 135). Clyde's lack of practical wisdom cannot be explained by his limited childhood training, however unrelated his parents' religious teachings seem to be to "the world." Like Alnashar, he "had a soul that was not destined to grow up. He lacked decidedly that mental clarity and inner directing application that in so many permits them to sort out from the facts and avenues of life the particular thing or things that make for their direct advancement" (I, 174). The seeming inevitability of Clyde's failure depends upon our accepting the fact that he never learns from his experience, that he remains the adolescent dreamer into his twenties.

The third story of *The Arabian Nights* which has relevance to the novel is the "History of the Fisherman" who on the third cast of his nets into the sea brings up a jar from which, when it is unsealed, a black smoke issues into the shape of a genie, or efrit. The efrit has power to reward the fisherman for releasing it, but unaccountably proceeds to threaten the fisherman with death; finally the fisherman tricks the efrit into returning to the jar for

---

little wild in thinking of it all. Once he and she were married, what could Sondra's relatives do? What, but acquiesce and take them into the glorious bosom of their resplendent home . . . he to no doubt eventually take some place in connection with the Finchley Electric Sweeper Company. And then would he not be . . . joint heir with Stuart to all the Finchley means" (II, 8).

a moment, and stoppers the jar with Solomon's seal forever. Clyde
is neither so suspicious nor so resourceful as the fisherman. He is
faced with a need to rid himself of Roberta Alden, who blocks his
acquisition of Sondra as "the central or crowning jewel to so much
sudden and such Aladdin-like splendor" (II, 8). Then he reads a
newspaper account of a double drowning in another state just
before he drives to a lake with Sondra and her friends. The con-
junction of these three events is enough to bring forth "as the
genii at the accidental rubbing of Aladdin's lamp—as the efrit
emerging as smoke from the mystic jar in the net of the fisherman
—the very substance of some leering and diabolic wish or wisdom
concealed in his own nature" (II, 48). Dreiser combines the language of *The Arabian Nights*, Freudian psychology, and Christian
theology as he personifies Clyde's "darker or primordial and unre-
generate nature" and "his darkest and weakest side" as a "Giant
Efrit . . . the Efrit of his own darker self," speaking in the "sealed
and silent hall" of his brain in language ambiguously like that of
the inscriptions on the walls of his parents' mission, "Behold! I
bring you a way. It is the way of the lake" (II, 49–56). Before
this "genii of his darkest and weakest side" Clyde seems powerless
to stopper the jar of his secret wishes or to drive them away with
his will.

Because he suggests "the way of the lake" (II, 53), the ambiguity of this genie is all the more terrifying. The life of the turbulent
sea which surrounded Carrie and Cowperwood was unambiguous;
it was a dangerous actuality, however unpredictable. Clyde, however, tries not so much to find a safe harbor from stormy seas as to
find a place on a lake which will not change its character beneath
him. It will be noticed that Clyde's love affairs are frequently
prosecuted on water. He comes nearest to intimacy with Hortense
Briggs (whose dream is a beaver coat) on the ice of a river near
Excelsior Springs. When he arrives in Lycurgus, he soon begins to
feel that his position as a Griffiths raises him above dancing to
"Dream Boat" with Rita Dickerman and Zella Shuman, and he
learns to swim, dive, and manage a canoe so that he will have the
accomplishments valued by the Griffiths and their friends. As he
paddles his canoe alone on Crum Lake, he discovers Roberta Alden
on the shore and takes her into his canoe to pick water lilies, but
even while he is on Crum Lake with Roberta he thinks that "had
fortune favored him in the first place by birth, he would now be in
some canoe on Schroon or Racquette or Champlain Lake with
Sondra Finchley or some such girl" (I, 263). Sondra, unlike

Roberta, is literally at home on the lake, in her family's new bungalow on Twelfth Lake, "right down at the water's edge" (I, 153), and she appears in a Lycurgus parade as an Indian maiden in a flower-covered canoe on the Mohawk (I, 241). To Clyde, Roberta soon comes to symbolize everything associated with his unhappy past—poverty, naiveté, sensuality warring with an uncertain primness, at best Crum Lake; Sondra, on the other hand, suggests wealth, sophistication, an easy confident manner, the social climate of Twelfth Lake. Dreiser catches this opposition in a single image: outside the Griffiths factory where Roberta stamps collars and where Clyde is assistant foreman is the river; "through the many open windows that reached from floor to ceiling could be seen the Mohawk swirling and rippling. . . . always [seeming] to hint of pleasures which might be found by idling along its shores" (I, 243).

How is Clyde to rid himself of Roberta and get Sondra? "Because of his own great interest in . . . any form of water life" (II, 23), he is attracted to the newspaper story of the accidental drowning of a couple on Pass Lake, Massachusetts. Some days later, after a trip to Big Bittern Lake with Sondra and her friends, Clyde meets his "genii," the embodiment of his overwhelming desire to do away with Roberta: "Would you escape from the demands of Roberta that but now and unto this hour have appeared unescapable to you? Behold! I bring you a way. It is the way of the lake—Pass Lake" (II, 49). The way of Pass Lake, enacted on Big Bittern Lake, will be, Clyde thinks, the way for him to pass forever from Crum Lake to Twelfth Lake.

As Clyde, the witless Aladdin, stumbles toward a seeming solution to his troubles, taking Roberta up the Mohawk to Utica, then on to Grass Lake, and finally to Big Bittern Lake, his life becomes more nightmare than actuality. He leaves such obvious clues behind him that a country lawyer can arrest him forty-eight hours from the time that Roberta's body is discovered. It is not simply that Clyde is stupid or inept (he has considerable success in his relationships with Sondra and her friends); rather he is moving *in* a dream and *toward* a dream of release and oblivion. When he takes Roberta into the boat on Big Bittern Lake, he recalls the details of their first outing on Crum Lake, but *this* lake and *this* Roberta are unreal: "an almost nebulous figure, she now seemed, stepping down into an insubstantial rowboat upon a purely ideational lake." The lake itself is magically shifting in shape. Behind an island the lake seemed to contain another lake within it, "an especially arranged pool or tarn to which one who was weary of life and cares—anxious to be away from the strife and contentions of the world, might most wisely and yet gloomily repair . . . where there was no end of anything—no plots—no plans—no practical problems to be solved—nothing. . . . the water itself looking like a huge black pearl cast by some mighty hand, in anger possibly, in sport or phantasy maybe" (II, 70, 74).

The Way of the Lake proves illusory for Clyde. The Big Bittern is a real lake, composed of real water which remains on his suit even when he carries it in his bag to Twelfth Lake. The lake does not accept Roberta into nothingness, but gives her up on a grappling hook along with Clyde's camera containing the snapshots that he had taken of her just before her drowning. The Way of the Lake does not make Sondra secure for Clyde: he never sees her again after his arrest, and the few hours he has with her before his arrest are filled with suffering as he watches her play at drowning in her boat on Twelfth Lake. Clyde's trial is not so much an unjust dispensing of "justice," as some of Dreiser's critics have suggested, as it is an indication of how inexorably the world moves on, how far it is removed from a fairy tale. Clyde's killing of Roberta was an actual killing, not a magic way to success. His world was a world in which his actions were related to others, not merely existing in isolation. "How people seemed to remember things," Clyde marvels during his trial, "more than ever he would have dreamed they would have" (II, 229).

Robert Shafer

An American Tragedy

Certainly . . . *An American Tragedy* is by all odds the best of Mr. Dreiser's novels, though perhaps not the most *interesting*. In it his language is still faulty, as in his earlier books; the

From *Humanism and America,* ed. Norman Foerster (New York: Farrar & Rinehart, 1930), pp. 161-69. All rights reserved. Reprinted by permission of Holt, Rinehart and Winston, Inc.

quality of his style is mediocre, when not worse; his narrative is badly proportioned;—but, nevertheless, the novel also has excellences which its author had not previously achieved, and which are seldom to be found save in works of a serious and mature artistry. It has a sombre inevitableness, a self-contained adequacy, a restraint, dignity, and detachment which bespeak not merely the experienced craftsman, but also the workman's sure grasp of his theme united with a deeply emotional confidence in its truth and importance. A far higher intelligence is exhibited in its execution than in Mr. Dreiser's play, *The Hand of the Potter* (1918), whose theme is similar in several respects. If one should name a single change indicative of the intelligent masterliness of *An American Tragedy*, perhaps the most significant is the fact that in this book, for the first time, Mr. Dreiser has permitted his characters and events to speak entirely for themselves.

But though *An American Tragedy* marks a really notable advance in technique, and a heightened plausibility thus attained, partly through restraint, still, it exhibits Mr. Dreiser's thought and the essential quality of his realism entirely unchanged. How Mr. Dreiser reached a mechanistic naturalism has above been shown, and how he became conscious of the fact. The appropriate result was that all his novels became tales of human irresponsibility, constructed to illustrate life's contradiction of the hollow conventions of society, and life's obedience to blind laws which make the individual's experience a chaos with an end unrelated to desert. This is the theme of *An American Tragedy*, as of the earlier novels. It is a tale of human irresponsibility, supported by youthful prejudices never relinquished, built up on false antitheses, and capped by a merely circumstantial realism calculated to give the narrative a deceptive air of importance.

Youthful prejudice, for example, transparently dictates the important part played by religion in this novel. Religion is represented as an illusion capable of deceiving only those blind to life's realities—the hopelessly incompetent and unintelligent, those whose advocacy would itself discredit any doctrine. Religion's illusory nature is said to be self-evident, indeed, since it has much to say of Providence, yet manifestly bestows on the convert no worldly rewards, in satisfaction of the real needs and desires with which he is endowed, not by his own design or wish. Convention, too, is represented as a force which sways only the stupid and lethargic, which makes no demands entitling it to respect, and which the intelligent disregard deliberately, the temperamental wilfully. Intelligence itself is pictured as merely an instrument useful for devising methods of self-advancement;—in other words, as the servant of inborn temperament. And temperament is the one irresistible, compelling force in life, to which all else is ultimately obedient. Hence no one is really responsible for anything;—save, perhaps, the novelist who sees this important truth, at length, and by careful selection of appropriate matter is able to picture it for us.

Not even Mr. Dreiser's expert care and long practice, however, are sufficient to enable him to evade a difficulty inherent in the nature of his theme. For the predicament of Roberta Alden is infinitely sad, and her creator narrates her history and murder with an exemplary truthfulness which emphasises that sadness to the full. Nevertheless, the reader's sympathy is not invoked. The girl, on the contrary, is presented as the inevitable resultant of inheritance, environment, and sex, and she lives as an embodied energy rather than as a person. Extraordinary pains are taken, with all the multitudinous details of her story, to balance causes against effects, and she emerges a plausible creature. There is nothing incredible in her being just conventional enough and unwary enough and love-sick enough to suit the story's purpose; but, too, there is nothing in her nature or her history to render either important. Indeed, her grievous distress, leading up to her murder, takes on, under Mr. Dreiser's hand, the same significance as the squirming of an angleworm, impaled by some mischievous boy—no less, but certainly no more.

"Chemic compulsion" draws Roberta Alden as it draws other substances. "Chemic compulsion" epitomises the book. It "just happens"—and this is all—that "chemic compulsion" entangles Roberta with the squid—Clyde Griffiths, the defeated squid. For readers of Mr. Dreiser's "epic" tale, *The Financier*, who recall the apologue of the lobster and the squid cannot fail to recognise Clyde Griffiths as the embodiment of the latter—and his cousin Gilbert as the patient, triumphant lobster. The squid, it need scarcely be said, commands no more sympathy than Roberta;—indeed, most readers inevitably must sympathise with the spirit of the "irate woodsman's" brutal question during the trial. This undefiled son of the forest asked: "Why don't they kill the God-damned bastard and be done with him?" But, just for this reason, it has to be remembered that Mr. Dreiser exhausts every possible means so to account for Clyde as to preserve him from all blame. The squid is the complete plaything of "chemic compulsion," the paragon of irresponsibility, the perfect exemplar of the truth as the truth has been revealed to his creator.

This being so, it is little less than a miracle that Mr. Dreiser has contrived—through the infinite detail of a merely circumstantial realism—to save Clyde Griffiths' humanity sufficiently to maintain the reader's "suspension of disbelief" until the end of the book. Undoubtedly he has done so, though he has not succeeded in making all readers feel that patience has been adequately rewarded. They have been impressed, as is fitting before so monumental a composition; they have been troubled; they have not been recompensed. Eight hundred and forty pages devoted to the unconscionable prolongation of a mere sensational newspaper story! Remarks to this effect I have heard more than once; and they roughly indicate the real difficulty—the inevitably self-destroying effect of such an effort as Mr. Dreiser's, in proportion as it is successful.

This difficulty, however, does not actually lie in the plot of *An American Tragedy*, as the remark just cited implies. The bare plot of the *Agamemnon* of Æschylus might equally well form the basis of a mere sensational newspaper story, and Clytæmnestra in that play and in the *Choephori* makes for herself, not without seeming justice, the plea that is made for Clyde Griffiths. Not she, but Destiny, she says, through her its helpless instrument slew Agamemnon; and she also pleads that she did not make herself, yet can only act out her inborn nature. But it is not for his plots, nor because he was well acquainted with Mr. Dreiser's view of life, that Æschylus lives on still amongst us. His dramas have a perennial and deep value for mankind because, rejecting the plausible notion of "chemic compulsion," he struggled with profound conviction to convey a very different meaning through their form, characters, and action. Without evading any of its difficulty, he asserted his faith that Moral Law uncompromisingly governs the life of man, making for an order which is divine, in the face of a chaos intrinsically evil, and that men are fully, if tragically, responsible for the consequences of their acts, whatever their motives or compulsions, so that ignorance and self-conceit are equally as criminal as violence.

This is not to say all, of course, but it may suffice to show how Æschylus and, more clear-sightedly, Sophocles cut straight through to the centre of the human problem and propounded a solution which, if not the only one, nor by itself a complete one, is still, strictly speaking, irrefutable, being founded directly upon facts of

experience which have not changed with the passing genera-
tions;—an unassailable solution, moreover, which gives weight and
meaning to every individual and to all of his acts. And hence it is
that the bloody and sensational fables of Æschylus and Sophocles,
triumphantly formed in full harmony with their meaning, have an
interest and value for men which time does not exhaust.

Mr. Dreiser's difficulty is not that he has different facts of
experience to interpret;—he has precisely the same facts concerning an essentially unchanged human nature. His difficulty is that
his mechanistic naturalism compels him so to select and mani-
pulate facts of experience as to deny, through his narrative, that
human life has any meaning or value. The attempt is suicidal, and
the more consistently it is carried out the more completely is
Mr. Dreiser forced to divest his creatures and their actions of any
distinctively human quality and meaning. The more successful he
is the more insignificant his work becomes. *An American Tragedy*,
as I have said, is more skilfully, faithfully, and consistently executed on the naturalistic level than any of its author's earlier
novels, and precisely for this reason it contains no single element
of tragedy in any legitimate sense of the word, and it impresses
thoughtful readers as a mere sensational newspaper story long
drawn out. In other words, in proportion as Mr. Dreiser contrives
to accomplish his self-imposed task he has nothing to tell us
except that there is nothing to tell about life until it can be
reduced even below the apparent level of animal existence, to the
point where it becomes a meaningless chaos of blind energies.

Whether or not any real sense of the self-destroying character
of this effort, to create a literature as valueless and insignificant
as possible, will ever strike Mr. Dreiser's consciousness, I should
not venture to guess. But only an obstinate self-conceit, or an
invincible stupidity, one imagines, could have kept him from seeing
the absurdities into which he was forced, in the course of half-a-
dozen sentences, when he recently attempted to draw up a brief
statement of his present belief. He wrote: "I can make no comment on my work or my life that holds either interest or import
for me. Nor can I imagine any explanation or interpretation of
any life, my own included, that would be either true—or important, if true. Life is to me too much a welter and play of inscrutable forces to permit, in my case at least, any significant comment. One may paint for one's own entertainment, and that of
others—perhaps. As I see him the utterly infinitesimal individual
weaves among the mysteries a floss-like and wholly meaningless

course—if course it be. In short I catch no meaning from all I have seen, and pass quite as I came, confused and dismayed."[1]

To this point has Mr. Dreiser's naturalism driven him. If the general sense of this awkward yet mannered statement comprised the truth about him and his work, he would, of course, never have been asked to make it. He would, in all probability, have been confined long ago to an asylum; and he would certainly never have written any of his books. Those books, moreover, have manifestly not been written just for his own entertainment. They have been written because he felt he had something to say—because of his certainty that he had come to know the truth, as men in general knew it not. And with singular faithfulness of purpose and of industry, involving what for him must have been almost superhuman effort, because of his defects of mind and training, he has devoted himself to the struggle to express the truth as he conceived it—that is, to reduce it to consistency and give it coherent form. He has also neglected nothing, within his limits, to make it impressive. He has thus lived a rationally purposive life, reducing at least to symptoms of order the welter of his impressions and impulses, controlling at least fitfully his rebellious temperament, and mastering (or "sublimating") at least partially his almost pathological obsession by sex. For the sake of self-expression—or, as I shall presently suggest, of self-justification—he has thus achieved an appreciably disciplined life, and so has in his own person, against his own literary aim, furnished a convincing refutation of his philosophy. He has effectively proved that *An American Tragedy* gives form to a view of life as gratuitous as it is unmeaning.

Fortunately it is now realised by an increasing number of people that naturalistic philosophies are merely speculative ventures, which derive no valid support from "modern science." And it has, besides, been shown above how little "science" had to do with the formation of Mr. Dreiser's naturalistic prejudice. Mr. Dreiser, on his own showing, was first awakened to a sense of life as a problem to be solved by his discovery of the radical contrast between the ethical standards of his father and his church (as he understood its teaching), and his own spontaneous impulses and desires. His haphazard, undirected education gave him an unexcelled opportunity to learn that there were many others like himself, that they seemed to be the most vigorous members of their

---

[1] From the *Bookman,* September, 1928 (Vol. 68, p. 25).

munities, and that they never hesitated to transgress every ethical standard, when they could get away with it, in their struggle for self-advancement and self-gratification. He treasured every impression which seemed to be on his side against ethical standards by which he stood condemned. His self-esteem had been gravely shocked by the discordance he had discovered, and he now found the means to restore it and, indeed, to strengthen it, by appeal from home and church to the larger world. Not he was in the wrong of it, but the "senseless," "impossible" theories which would have convicted him of shameful tendencies. "In shame there is no comfort, but to be beyond all bounds of shame," says one of Sidney's Arcadians, and this Mr. Dreiser might thenceforth have taken for his motto.

Governed by this apolaustic prejudice, he has since continued his transparent course of seeing only what he has desired to see, or rather of admitting the reality of only what has suited him, while setting down all else as either hypocrisy or delusion. And while it is true that no one escapes the necessity of bringing only a selective attention to bear upon the outer world, it by no means follows that we are all alike cut off from "reality." On the contrary, it does mean that the basis of our selective attention, the interests and purposes served by it, are of fundamental importance. And the disastrous effect of Mr. Dreiser's apolaustic prejudice is that it encouraged him in slavery to mere temperament, in helpless surrender to the chaotic flow of "natural" impulses, while it brought to his attention from the outer world only what fed itself, the antics of complicated beasts with strange illusions. The trouble with what he thus saw is not that it was non-existent, some gross trick of the fevered imagination;—it was there to be seen—it is there, in grievous plenty. No, the trouble is that none of it has positive significance. The naturalism which it fathers lights up the animal in man, but tells man nothing of that which positively distinguishes him from the beast—more, it vindictively denies that anything save hypocrisy and delusion does so distinguish him. And while it seeks to dissolve our humanity, it ends, as it ends in Mr. Dreiser, in a bottomless morass of misrepresentation and despair. This is the American tragedy of our confused age which constitutes the real import of Mr. Dreiser's masterpiece.

NOTE—For permission to quote from the writings of Mr. Dreiser, I am indebted both to him and to his publisher, Mr. Horace Liveright.

An American Tragedy

Theodore Dreiser once said that his philosophy of love might be called "Varietism." But there was one mistress to whom he remained faithful, after his fashion, all his life. That mistress was the bitch-goddess Success. He knew all her failings and falsities. He knew that her sweetest kiss would turn to dust on the tongue. But he could never forget her face. And all his stories are about her.

Dreiser was born in Terre Haute, Indiana, in 1871, of an immigrant German father and an illiterate Moravian mother. The father was a Catholic, pious, rigid, and totally incompetent, "a thin grasshopper of a man, brooding wearily." The mother was warmhearted and full of unjudging sympathy for the defeated, maimed, and erring, but had little capacity to make up for the father's practical failure. Dreiser knew a boyhood of poverty, ignorance, rejection, sad yearnings, and grandiose daydreams. In his youth he was, as he says in his autobiography, "blazing with sex, as well as with a desire for material and social supremacy," but his anger at the frustration of this "materialistic lust of life" was sometimes transmuted into a pity for others deprived like himself, for "life in all its helpless degradation and poverty, the unsatisfied dreams of people." He saw that pain is pain, even when it is pain at the frustration of unworthy desire. He saw, for instance, his father's impotence in the face of the booming economic system he could never understand; he saw one brother jailed for forgery, and another hit the road to die, by the time he was forty, of dissipation and defeat; he saw one sister early seduced by a political big-shot of Terre Haute, and later another sister come home to give birth to an illegitimate child.

But Dreiser, still a boy, saw also the brother who had been jailed turn up as Paul Dresser, a successful song-writer and theatre man, elegant in a fur coat, to snatch the family out of starvation and establish them in a house owned by his current sweetheart—the prototype of Sal in his song "My Gal Sal" and a successful whore-momma of Evansville, Indiana.

Reprinted from *The Yale Review*, LII (October 1962), 1-15, by permission of William Morris Agency, Inc. Copyright © 1962 by Robert Penn Warren.

And the young Dreiser, who saw the fur coat and silk hat of Paul Dresser, was soon to see the rambunctious, brutal energy of Chicago on the make. So success was possible, too. Dreiser was, in fact, the child of the Gilded Age, but the gilding he knew was the glitter of gaslight on rhinestone, red plush, and saloon art; and this glitter remained, in one part of his being, the image of the highest beauty, even when, in some of the novels, the glitter of rhinestone is officially replaced by the cold fire of the diamond and the saloon art by genuine oils attributed to Bouguereau.

Into the worship of success entered another notion—the notion, derived from observation and from reading Balzac, Zola, Spencer, and Huxley, that life is merely the blind collision of "accidental, indifferent, and bitterly cruel forces." In this world the virtues of neither Christianity nor Horatio Alger could be closely depended upon to prevail. But there was something worse than the prospect of surrendered virtue. Of his discovery of Huxley and Spencer, he says: "Up to this time there had been in me a blazing and unchecked desire to get on, the feeling that in doing so we did get somewhere; now in its place was the definite conviction that spiritually one got nowhere. . . ."

One got nowhere, there was blankness; but for all men there was, nevertheless, the doom of desire, the compulsion blazing unchecked and beyond the tutelage of any philosophy; and for Dreiser himself that doom was compounded by a second, the doom of having to record the saga of desire and thus relive its pathos.

Dreiser's saga of desire has two forms. The first form is the story of the superman, like Cowperwood of *The Titan* and *The Financier* or Witla of *The Genius*, the brutal realist who sees through the shams of the world and ruthlessly applies the force of his own superior "chemism"—to use another of Dreiser's infelicitous words, like "varietism"—in that collision of "bitterly cruel forces" which is life. In these stories, we find some documentary value, the value of old photographs and newspaper clippings, the color of a period, the shock that the idea of the survival of the fittest made on the old-fashioned world, a notion of what some of the Titans and Geniuses of the period may have thought, in their deepest selves, of themselves, and even moments of dramatic force. But all in all, there is a dreary and mechanical repetitiousness in these tales of the triumph of superior "chemisms" in the collision of "accidental, indifferent, and bitterly cruel forces."

Here we see the stultifying effects of Dreiser's philosophy when directly applied to the materials of life. The trouble, let us hasten to say, does not lie in the basic nature of the philosophy itself. Dreiser's philosophy, though crudely put and grossly naked of any decent professional draperies, is but another example of nineteenth-century materialism—the vision of the God-abandoned and sanction-stripped world of natural process. The trouble, for fiction at least, is not even that Dreiser has no subtle dialectic to develop the logical implications of the vision. The trouble is the spirit in which Dreiser applies the idea to the materials of life. The ideas of Zola or Hardy are not, at root, greatly different from those of Dreiser. The difference between *Nora* or *Tess* and *The Titan* is the spirit in which the ideas are related to experience. This is a spirit that tends to schematize those materials deductively, to delimit arbitrarily the range of human experience, to deny the constructive and idealizing function of imagination in his characters and, in the end, in himself.

There is, furthermore, another kind of trouble in these tales of success. Dreiser, looking back on the life-hating God of his grasshopper-thin, brooding father, and hating that father for his life-failure, could, in part of his being, vindictively rejoice in the death of God, and vicariously fulfill, in the triumph of his Lucky Jims, those energies which he had feared that God and the father, in their several ways, had robbed him of. The vindictive rejoicing and the vicarious fulfilment combine to deprive these stories of emotional resonance. These qualities, despite the scrupulous documentation, infect the work with abstraction. They give, instead of the richness and suggestiveness of life, an impression of dreary compulsion and mechanical repetition. Ultimately we miss the human awareness. These tales of success are, we may say, the work done under the aegis of the father; and they fail.

The second form of the saga of desire is the stories of failure; and they do not fail. *Sister Carrie, Jennie Gerhart,* and *An American Tragedy* are the work done, to pursue our conceit, under the aegis of the mother. Something of that unjudging warmth of heart which Dreiser reports of her enables him to transmute the bitterness of his own recollected failures and chronic fears of the future into a tenderness toward creatures doomed, for whatever reason, to fail. His approach is not deductive here; he lives, and relives, their failure. The "chemisms" may blindly and cruelly collide and the great machine of the universe grind blankly on, but the fact

of the blindness and blankness of the process does not abolish the
pain of a victim. Nor does it abolish that mysterious sense of
triumph which Jennie Gerhart feels at the end of her story, in the
midst of her failure. It may be argued that Sister Carrie herself
does not "fail," that she rises in the world. But her success is as
much a part of the world of blind accident as is Hurstwood's failure, and the image of Carrie at the end, in her rocking chair, is
the image of someone who, in getting somewhere, has gone nowhere.

In these tales the human awareness is set over against the
natural process of which the human creature is a part, and the
unresolvable paradox of that confrontation is the drama. It is
the drama in which we all live—or at least the drama which we
must take as a starting point for whatever our interpretation of
our living and whatever effort to resolve the paradox. It is the
drama, too, in which Dreiser's imagination stirs to life.

Dreiser's tales of failure are his successes, and *An American
Tragedy*, in which failure is unalleviated, is his greatest success.
Published in 1925, it is the work in which he could look backward
from the distance of middle-age and evaluate his own experience of success and failure. We feel, in this book, the burden of
the personal pathos, the echo of the personal struggle to purge the
unworthy aspirations. We also feel, in this book, the burden of a
historical moment, the moment of the Great Boom which climaxed
the period from Grant to Coolidge, the half century in which the
new America of industry and finance capitalism was hardening
into shape and its secret forces were emerging to dominate all life.
In other words, *An American Tragedy* can be taken as a document,
both personal and historical, and it is often admired, and defended,
in these terms.

As a document it is indeed powerful, but such documentary
power is derivative: an artifact dug from the Sumerian tomb
moves us whether it is beautiful or not simply because some human hand, nameless and long since dust, had fashioned it; and a
book may move us because we know what, of a man's life or of a
moment in history, it represents. But the power of *An American
Tragedy* is not derivative. The weight of Dreiser's experience and
of the historical moment are here, but they are here as materials;
in the strange metabolism of creation, they are absorbed and
transmuted into fictional idea, fictional analogy, fictional illusion.

The book is "created," and therefore generates its own power, multiplying the power implicit in the materials.

The thing in *An American Tragedy* most obviously created is Clyde Griffiths himself. The fact that Dreiser, in his characteristic way, chose a model for Clyde—one Chester Gillette, who, in 1906, had drowned his sweetheart, Grace Brown, in Moose Lake, Herkimer County, N. Y.—does not make Clyde less of a creation. Rather, it emphasizes that he is a creation; and the contrast between the dreary factuality of an old newspaper account and the anguishing inwardness of the personal story may well have served as a mirror for the contrast that always touched Dreiser's feelings and fired his imagination—the contrast between the grinding impersonality of the machine of the world and the pathos of the personal experience. In fact, the novel begins and ends with an image of this contrast: the family of street preachers, in the beginning with the boy Clyde and in the end with the illegitimate son of Clyde's sister Esta, stand lost between the "tall walls of the commercial heart of an American city" and lift up their hymn "against the vast skepticism and apathy of life." The image of the boy Clyde looking up at the "tall walls" of the world is the key image of the novel.

The creation of the character of Clyde is begun by a scrupulous accretion of detail, small indications, and trivial events. We are early caught in the dawning logic of these details. We see the sidewise glances of yearning. We see how, when he discovered his sister Esta in the secret room, pregnant and abandoned, his first reaction is selfish; how only when she refers to "poor Mamma" does his own sympathy stir; how this sympathy is converted suddenly into a sense of world-pathos, and then, in the end, turns back into self-pity. We see him staring at the rich house of his uncle, and again when for the first time he lays eyes on Sondra, with "a curiously stinging sense of what it was to want and not to have." We see his real sadness at Roberta's jealousy, which he, also one of the deprived, can feel himself into, but we know that his pity for her is, at root, self-pity. We see him open the *Times-Union* to see the headline: *Accidental Double Tragedy at Pass Lake*. We see all this, and so much more, and remember his mother's letter to him after his flight from Kansas City: ". . . for well I know how the devil tempts and pursues all of us mortals, and particularly just such a child as you." And what a stroke it is to fuse the reader's foreboding interest with the anxiety of the mother!

For Dreiser's method of presenting the character is far deeper
and more subtle than that of mere accretion. The method is an
enlargement and a clarifying, slow and merciless, of a dimly envisaged possibility. We gradually see the inward truth of the
mother's clairvoyant phrase, "such a child as you"; and the story
of Clyde Griffiths is the documentation of this.

A thousand strands run backward and forward in this documentation, converting what is a process in time into a logic outside
of time. When back in Kansas City, we see Clyde's sexual fear and
masochism in relation to the cold, cunning Hortense, we are laying
the basis for our understanding of what will come later, the repetition with Sondra of the old relationship and the avenging of it on
the defenseless Roberta. When in the room of women where Clyde
is foreman, he looks wistfully out the window on the summer
river, we are being prepared for the moment when he first encounters Roberta at the pleasure lake, and for the grimmer
moment to come on Big Bittern Lake. When, on the night after
the first meeting with Sondra, Clyde does not go to Roberta, we
know that this is a shadowy rehearsal for the last betrayal and
murder.

It is not only that we find, in an analytic sense, the logic of
character displayed; in such instances we find this logic transliter-
ated into a thousand intermingling images, and in this transliteration the logic itself becoming the poetry of destiny. We see the
process moving toward climax when, on the train, on the death
ride with Roberta, Clyde flees from his own inner turmoil into the
objective observations which, in their irrelevancy, are the mark
of destiny: *Those nine black and white cows on that green hillside*,
or *Those three automobiles out there running almost as fast as the
train*. And we find the climax of the process in the "weird, con-
temptuous, mocking, lonely" call of the weir-weir bird which offers
a commentary on the execution, as it had on the birth, of the
murderous plan.

This transliteration of logic into a poetry of destiny is what
accounts for our peculiar involvement in the story of Clyde. What
man, short of saint or sage, does not understand, in some secret
way however different from Clyde's way, the story of Clyde and
does not find it something deeper than a mere comment on the
values of American culture? Furthermore, the mere fact that our
suspense is not about the *what* but about the *how* and the *when*
emphasizes our involvement. No, to be more specific, our *entrapment*. We are living out a destiny, painfully waiting for a doom.
We live into Clyde's doom, and in the process live our own secret

sense of doom which is the backdrop of our favorite dramas of the will.

How deep is our involvement—or entrapment—is indicated by the sudden sense of lassitude, even relief, once the murder is committed; all is now fulfilled, and in that fact the drawstring is cut. So we may even detach ourselves, at least for the moment, from the youth now "making his way through a dark, uninhabited wood, a dry straw hat upon his head, a bag in his hand . . ."

As a commentary on Dreiser's art, we can note how, after this sentence that closes Book II, Dreiser jerks back his camera from that lonely figure and begins Book III by withdrawing into magisterial distance for a panoramic sweep of the lens: "Cataraqui County extending from the northernmost line of the village known as Three Mile Bay on the south to the Canadian border, on the north a distance of fifty miles. Its greater portion covered by uninhabited forests and . . ." The whole effect is that of detachment; and with this we are restored, after a long painful while, to the role of observer, uninterested and critical, not involved.

But we shall not be long permitted to keep this comfortable role. Soon the camera will come close to the cell where Clyde waits, the focus will be sharpened. And in this alternation of focus, and shift from involvement to detachment, we find one of the deep art-principles of the work, one of the principles of its compelling rhythm. It is compelling because the shift of focus is never arbitrary; it grows out of the expressive needs of the narrative as Dreiser has conceived it, and out of the prior fact that the narrative is conceived in a drama between the individual and the universe.

Randolph Bourne once said that Dreiser had the "artist's vision without the sureness of the artist's technique." This is true of most of Dreiser's books, and in a limited sense may be true of *An American Tragedy*. I have used the phrase "Dreiser's art" in full awareness that most critics, even critics as dangerous to disagree with as Lionel Trilling, will find it absurd; and in full awareness that even those who admire Dreiser will, with few exceptions, concede a point on "art," or apologetically explain that Dreiser's ineptitudes somehow have the value of stylistic decorum and can be taken as a manifestation of his groping honesty, and will then push on to stake their case on his "power" and "compassion."

But ultimately how do we know the "power" or the "compassion"—know them differently, that is, from the power or compassion we may read into a news story—except by Dreiser's

control? Except, in other words, by his grasp of the human materials and his rhythmic organization of them, the vibrance which is
the life of fictional illusion, that mutual interpenetration in meaning of part and whole which gives us the sense of preternatural
fulfillment? Except, in short, by art?

There is a tendency to freeze the question of Dreiser as an
artist at the question of prose style. As for prose style, Dreiser is
a split writer. There is the "literary" writer whose style is abomi-
nable. But there is another writer, too, a writer who can write a
scene with fidelity if not always with felicity. But sometimes there
is the felicity, a felicity of dramatic baldness: the letters of Mrs.
Griffiths or Roberta; the scene of Roberta back home, in her
mother's house, looking out at the ruined fields; or the scene when
Clyde first sees Sondra, with that "curiously stinging sense of what
it is to want and not to have."

Words are what we have on the page of a novel, and words are
not only a threshold, a set of signs, but a fundamental aspect of
meaning, absorbed into everything else. Words, however, are not
the only language of fiction. There is the language of the unfolding
scenes, the language of the imagery of enactment, with all its
primitive massiveness—the movie in our heads, with all the entailed
questions of psychological veracity and subtlety, of symbolic densi-
ties and rhythmic complexities. I am trying here to indicate something of the weight of this language, or better, languages, as an
aspect of Dreiser's art.

With this intention we can return to the question of the rhythm
between detachment and involvement, which manifests itself in
shifts of pace and scale. But we may find the basis for another
rhythm in the fact that the personal story of Clyde is set in a
whole series of shifting perspectives. By perspective I do not mean
a point of view in the ordinary technical sense. I mean what may
be called an angle of interest. For instance, the picture of the
organization of the collar factory in Lycurgus gives a perspective
on life, and on the fate of Clyde; this is another contrast between
a mechanism and man, a symbolic rendering of the ground idea
of the novel.

But there are many perspectives. There is the perspective of the
religious belief of the family, which returns in the end to frame
the whole story; that of the world of the bell-hop's bench in the
hotel; that of sex and "chemism"; that of the stamping room in
the factory with its mixture of sex, social differences, power, and
money; that of the economic order of Lycurgus which stands as a

mirror for the world outside; that of the jealousies and intrigues of the young social set of the town, jealousies and intrigues which, ironically enough, make it possible for Clyde to enter that charmed circle; that of justice and law in relation to the political structure of Cataraqui County; that of the death house.

Sometimes a perspective comes as an idea boldly stated, sometimes as implicit in a situation or person. In fact, all the persons of the novel, even the most incidental, are carriers of ideas and represent significant perspectives in which the story may be viewed. In the enormous cast there are no walk-ons; each actor has a role in the structure of the unfolding dialectic. And it is the pervasive sense of this participation, however unformulated, that gives the novel its density, the weight of destiny.

If, as a matter of fact, the dialectic were insisted upon as dialectic we should not find this weight. We find it only because the dialectic unfolds in personality, in the presentation of personality not as a carrier of idea but as a thing of inner vibrance. The mother, for instance, is a small masterpiece of characterization. She is the carrier of "religion," but with her own inner contradictions, exists in her full and suffering reality, a reality which, at the end when she comes to join Clyde, affirms itself by her effect on everyone around. Roberta is fully rendered, not only in her place in the social and economic order and in her role as victim, but with the complexity of her humanity. When her friend Grace catches her in a lie about Clyde, she stiffens with "resentment." She does not quite tell the truth to her mother about why she moves out of her first room. In the midst of her as yet submerged moral struggle she deceives even herself as to why she selects a room downstairs and with an outside door in the new house. She is a sufferer, but she is not beyond the flash of jealous anger when Clyde, with unconscious brutality, remarks that Sondra dresses well: "If I had as much money as that, I could too." And the scene in which Clyde tries to persuade her to let him come to her room is of extraordinary depth, coming to climax when he turns sullenly away, and she, overwhelmed by her fear and pain at her own rebelliousness, feels the "first, flashing, blinding, bleeding stab of love."

Even minor characters have more than their relation to the dialectic. The prosecuting attorney and the defending lawyers have their own depth, and their roles are defined by their personal histories. A character like Hortense may be merely sketched in, but she takes on a new significance when we see

her, like Rita, as an earlier avatar of Sondra, who is—and let us
dwell on the adjectives—"as smart and vain and sweet a girl as
Clyde had ever laid eyes on." And if at first Sondra herself seems
scarcely more than another example of the particular type of
femme fatale destined to work Clyde's ruin, let us remember
how Clyde, in his cell, receives the letter beginning: "Clyde—
This is so that you will not think someone once dear to you has
utterly forgotten you. . . ." The letter, typewritten, is unsigned,
but with it, in all the mixture of human feeling and falsity,
Sondra, retroactively as it were, leaps to life.

As every person enters the story with a role in the dialectic,
so every person enters with a human need which seeks fulfilment
in the story. The delineation of this need—for instance, the
portrait of the socially ambitious clerk in Lycurgus or the history
of the prosecuting attorney Mason—serves to distract our interest from Clyde's personal story, another kind of distancing of
the main line of narrative. At the same time, in the extraordinary coherence of the novel, we finally see that such apparent
digressions are really mirrors held up to Clyde's story, in fact to
Clyde himself: in this world of mirrors complicity is the common doom. So here we have—in the distraction of interest and
realization of complicity—another version of the rhythm of approach and withdrawal.

There is, indeed, another sense in which the delineation of
each new need compensates, in the end, for the distraction it
has provoked. Each new need serves as a booster to the thrust of
narrative, and in the rhythm of these thrusts we find another
principle of the organization of the whole. Or to change our
image, in the braiding together of these needs with the need of
Clyde, we find acceleration, the pulse of creative life. To put
it still another way, the delineation of each new perspective,
each new person, each new need acts as a kind of "unmasking"
of the dynamism of the story, in individual and social terms; and
something of our own resistance to unmasking enters into the
whole response to the story. This resistance, set against our
natural commitment to the narrative, creates another sort of
frustrating tension, and another sort of rhythm of withdrawal
and approach. Furthermore, over against the unmasking of the
mechanism of life is set the feel of life itself being lived in the
urgency of its illusions; and this contrast gives us, if we choose

to regard it as such, another principle of rhythm, another principle by which the form unfolds.

We have spoken of the marked moment of withdrawal at the beginning of Book III, after we have left Clyde walking away from the scene of Roberta's death, into the forest. Our commitment to the movement of narrative leading to the death of Roberta has been so complete that now, with it accomplished, we feel a sense of let-down, of the end. The sense of an end is so strong that the story of the now accomplished crime seems, for the moment at least, to split off from the subsequent story of consequences; and Dreiser, by the moment of withdrawal into distance, emphasizes the split. The split, coming about two-thirds of the way through the novel, has been felt, by some readers, as a grave flaw in the structure. The split is indeed real—a real break in emotional continuity. But we must ask ourselves whether or not this split serves, as the similar "split" in Conrad's *Lord Jim* or Shakespeare's *Julius Caesar*, to emphasize a deeper thematic continuity.

The story is one of crime and punishment. In the first two Books we see the forces that converge toward the death of Roberta, and in Book III we see the forces that are triggered into action by her death; that is, we see as a continuing theme the relation of the individual personality and individual fate to such forces. What, in other words, is the nature of responsibility in this world of shadowy complicities, where all things conspire in evil? The shadowiness of the outer world is matched by the shadowiness of the inner world; at the very last moment by the boat Clyde does not "will" to strike Roberta—even her death is an accident. Then after the "accident" this shadowiness of the inner world merges again with that of the outer. For instance, Jephson, one of the lawyers defending Clyde, creates a version of the accident; and then Clyde is persuaded, without much resistance, to testify to a "lie" in order to establish, as Jephson put it, the "truth."

This scene of the "persuasion" of Clyde is matched by a later scene in which, after Clyde's conviction, the young preacher McMillan strips Clyde of all his alibis and equivocations, and prepares him for repentance and salvation. But just before the execution, even as Clyde assures his mother that God has heard his prayers, he is asking himself: "Had he?" And Clyde goes to his death not knowing what he really knows or feels, or what he has done. The theme of complicity and ambiguity, in varying manifestations, runs throughout.

The fact that Dreiser divides the novel into only three Books falsifies the real structure. There are really four basic movements, and there should be four Books: the story up to the flight from Kansas City, the story of the preparation; the story of the temptation leading to the death of Roberta; the story of the conviction, that of the ambiguities of justice; and the story of the search for salvation as death draws near. And in the last phase another theme, related to the others but more deeply grounded, appears, the theme of identity. If in this world of complicities and ambiguities it is hard to understand responsibility, then how, ultimately, can one understand the self? In fact, in this world of shadows Clyde has always sought to flee from the self. In all his self-absorption and selfishness, he has sought to repudiate the deepest meaning of self. He had longed to enter the "tall walls" of the world and find there a dream-self, a self-to-be-created, a role to play in the rich and thrilling world—a role, we may say, to take the place of a self. The very end of Book I, which has described Clyde's first attempt to enter the world, shows him fleeing from the wreck of the borrowed car: ". . . he hoped to hide—to lose himself and so escape . . ." He wishes to escape responsibility and punishment; he does "lose himself," and early in Book II we learn that he has lost his name, to reassume it only when he can use it to advantage with his rich uncle from Lycurgus.

All the rest of Clyde's grim, sleazy story can be regarded as an attempt to repudiate the old self. And the repudiation of self is associated with Clyde's readiness to repudiate others: he is ashamed of his family; he drops new friends—Dillard and Rita, for example—as soon as he makes contact with his rich relations; he ends by murdering Roberta. Or it may be put that Clyde, having no sense of the reality of self, has no sense of the reality of others, and even his pity for others is always a covert self-pity.

At the end, in a last desperate hope, Clyde is forced by McMillan to face the truth that he has fled from responsibility and self. But even now, as Clyde tries to accept the self, he cannot be sure of who or what he is. His "tragedy" is that of namelessness, and this is one aspect of its being an American tragedy, the story of the individual without identity, whose responsible self has been absorbed by the great machine of modern industrial secularized society. I say "secularized" because the only persons who offer a notion of self that Dreiser can set against the machine of the world are Clyde's mother and the Reverend McMillan. This is not to say that Dreiser is offering a doctrinal solution, but it is to say that only in the image drawn from religion does he, ironically enough, with all his ambivalences, find an image of the responsible self.

Many critics, by way of blame or praise, have emphasized the mechanistic view informing Dreiser's work. Critics who make the emphasis by way of blame are usually referring to his notion of "chemisms," of blind forces in the blood. Those who do so by way of praise are usually referring to some notion of social determinism. James Farrell succinctly puts this view: "To him, evil is social: all his novels are concerned with social history, the social process of evil. Ambition, yearning, aspiration—these all revolve around this problem, and it in turn revolves around the role of money. He has related social causation . . . to the individual pattern of destiny."

He has indeed. And this fact is part of his great power and enduring importance as a novelist. But it is only a part, however original and essential a part. The real drama, which finally gives value to the whole and makes that greater than the sum of the parts, lies in the fact that in the full context of "social causation," as in that of the "chemisms," the individual story, in all its throbbing consciousness, is paradoxically and anguishingly enacted. The last anguish is the yearning for identity. And this yearning is the last mystery, the story in which Dreiser has, to use Mencken's words, "lifted the obvious to the inexplicable."